THE BOO

DREAMS

AN A-Z OF DREAM INTERPRETATION

Pamela J. Ball

ARCTURUS

ACKNOWLEDGMENTS

I would like to acknowledge the help I have received from various people. Firstly, I must pay due regard to the assistance from Andrew, who has lightened many a dull moment and done a large portion of the typing and research. I should also like to acknowledge help from James, Davina, Ann and Nikki and the many others drawn into the task of writing this book. Not least, do I thank my husband John for his support during some trying times.

ARCTURUS

This edition published in 2011 by Arcturus Publishing Limited
26/27 Bickels Yard, 151–153 Bermondsey Street,
London SE1 3HA

Copyright © 2002 Arcturus Publishing Limited
Abridged version of 'Your Dreams Interpreted'

ISBN: 978-1-84837-125-5
AD001101EN

Printed in Singapore

Why we dream

Dreams are said to be the mind's way of making sense of various types of sensory input with which it has to cope during ordinary day-to-day living. Mental and physical breakdown occurs very quickly without the relief of sleep and the dreaming process.

Dreams are thought to be a sort of self-cleaning, self-clearing process – a filing system which makes room each night for the next day's new information. During the waking day we are capable of assessing what is going on externally as well as internally and to make decisions and have insights in the light of fresh material that is being received. Both the incoming information and the insights are stored for later use by the mind and can – and often do – appear in dreams in an apparently random fashion. This store information is known as 'day's residue'.

In addition to ensuring that our brain sorts and files information correctly, dreams enable us to function successfully within the world in which we live by helping us to use that stored information effectively. Dreams allow us to select the best options from the store in whatever we are doing. The conscious logical mind places restrictions on our thought processes. When these are removed, the mind is free to roam wherever it pleases and, released from inhibition, will explore deeper, more creative layers of consciousness. The scenarios and situations that emerge while we dream often defy explanation. This is because we are tapping into both our own storehouse of images and into an even more subtle level of information that is available to everyone. This is the level that the Swiss psychoanalyst Carl Jung labelled 'Collective Unconscious'.

Interpreting dreams

Dreams often have to be interpreted from more than one perspective in order to be fully understood. Human beings are naturally holistic (that is, treatable as a whole person); dream interpretation cannot be an exact science and must take into account the dreamer's understanding of himself. Dream interpretation is like learning a new language, except that the actual basic language is a universal one and already known to us. As we become better acquainted with the language of dreams, a jumble of impressions gradually gains meaning and order and a medley of sound achieves some kind of significance. It is simply a matter of learning the various dialects.

The basic language of dream has common themes and widely accepted meanings, but we each have our own dialect which arises from our own experience, family stories, perceptions and emotions. The only interpretation which is truly valid is our own, though we can ask for help from others who speak the same language, or we can take the time to learn a new terminology.

Dealing with personal issues

Dreams will often highlight issues in our lives which need improving or changing. You may find certain key images occurring together in a dream will give you a clue as to the issues you need to address. the body and the mind will do their level best, both individually and together, to restore us to wellbeing and will, when necessary, use dreams to warn of impending difficulty or to present possible solutions. This type of dream occurs most often during times of illness, before or after surgery or after some life trauma, such as a family bereavement or job loss. It is as though the body and the mind are striving to re-establish an internal balance.

Aristotle recognised the possibility of a connection between how we dream and our wellbeing all of 2300 years ago. Hippocrates, the father of medicine, suggested that dreams were influenced by illness. Today, psychologists are aware that dreams can be affected by modern day medication – some of the common types of beta blocker, for example, are known to cause individuals to have lurid dreams, and this feature is given as one of the side effects.

Working with dreams

One of the interesting aspects of using dreams is that what may seem to be a physical problem – or the onset of one – can often be dealt with from an emotional or even a spiritual perspective. It is in these areas of our being that dreams and their interpretation can play a very effective part. By careful monitoring of your physical body, for instance, you may be able to recognise when physical difficulties are becoming a problem and take whatever remedial action you consider necessary. The more in tune with your body you are, the more quickly you will subconsciously recognise its needs. This awareness should enable you to instruct your dreaming self, before going to sleep, to give you a dream which will provide more specific information as to what you should do in order to deal with whatever problem your subconscious has identified.

Let us suppose that you have a physical problem which has proved difficult to treat – for example an ulcerated leg which will not heal. You may be trying all the appropriate physical remedies when action from a different perspective is what is really required. The symbolism of the ulcer may suggest that something is 'eating you up'. You might at this point need to look for a cause within your emotional make-up as to what the reason for this might be and what indeed that something is. You may need to spend sometime asking your dreaming self some questions. You could for instance, ask for a symbol which represents the ulcer, the emotion or the reason for the difficulty.

Because, without training, the dreaming self is somewhat unruly, it will often suggest multiple answers or possibly none at all! But being patient will eventually bring results. Your dreaming self has given you a very clear image of a way of working with the problem and opening the way for you to use subsequent dreams to clarify the process.

Dreams and the personality

Dreams and understanding ourselves are very closely interlinked. Through dreams we are able to put ourselves in touch with the hidden, unconscious parts of our personalities. We are capable then of altering our perception of a problem from within, rather than only dealing with the symptoms. For instance, something may have happened during childhood which we have buried deep within us. Only when a similar trauma happens in adult life does that part of us which knows and remembers everything look through its records and present the original trauma (often in symbolic form) for our consideration.

With some very basic knowledge of dream symbolism and imagery you should also be able to interpret other people's dreams as well as your own through the use of intuition.

Abandoned

Akin to the sense of being rejected, being abandoned is in many ways one of the first experiences we have as a human being. It represents a sense of how we experienced the first severance from our mother. How the child experiences this severance can traumatise it to the point where in later life that abandonment and severe sense of loss occurs in dreams. More positively, to be without restraint suggests – to act in an abandoned manner – a need for freedom.

Abortion

Abortion suggests the need for effort to get rid of what is no longer needed. One can reject a sensitivity, emotion, conviction or philosophy, which could be troublesome in some way. Abortion, being somewhat violent, can also indicate the sudden termination of a favourite project. In a woman's dream abortion can suggest some fear of childbirth.

Abyss

An abyss suggests that we recognise within ourselves the so called bottomless pit or void. There is a fear of losing control, of a loss of identity, or of some type of failure. We must take a risk without knowing what the outcome is going to be. More positively, it represents the possibility of reaching beyond our own boundaries or present experience. The abyss may also indicate our coming to terms with opposites such as right and wrong, good and bad.

Accident

Dreams of an accident suggests an element of the unexpected in some circumstance within our lives. We are usually receiving a warning or highlighting anxieties to do with safety or carelessness. It may be that we need to be aware of a lack of forethought in other people.

Acorn

Life, fertility and immortality are symbolised by the acorn, as is the androgynous. A huge growth process is starting to emerge from small beginnings. The germ of an idea is present but patience is needed. When such a fundamental symbol appears we are literally returning to our roots.

Actor

Dreaming of an actor suggests that we need to take responsibility for our actions and for who we are. Performers of one kind or another may also serve in dreams as a projection of the type of person we would like to be. We may, for instance, in real life be shy and withdrawn, but need to be admired and loved.

Addiction

We all have our own everyday needs, be it alcohol, drugs, exercise or anything that one feels that one can't do without. If we dream of being addicted, then some obsession needs to be acknowledged and action needs to be taken. A release of some kind is needed, be it from a substance, a person, or a certain situation. If one is not normally of an addictive personality, then perhaps the human pleasure seeking capabilities should be recognised. Fear of addiction in dreams suggests we have a fear of being swamped or overcome by someone or something.

Adolescent

Dreams of oneself as an adolescent concentrate on the undeveloped, perhaps immature, side of the personality. Dreaming of an adolescent of the opposite sex often means having to deal with a suppressed part of one's development. The emotions associated with adolescence are very raw and clear and to get back to such innocence is often possible only through dreams. There may be conflict over freedoms both given and taken by others.

Address

An address is usually a place of safety and security. However, the relevance of a particular address to the dreamer is probably significant. If that place was safe, then the dreamer is probably harking back to something from that period that is missing; if unhappy, the dreamer wants to escape from the past, and is being reminded of how he or she dealt with the situation. Comparisons are being drawn to enable the dreamer to act appropriately. A new address may suggest a radical change in life or circumstance.

Advertisement

There comes a time in all our lives when we need recognition for our efforts – being aware of advertisements in dreams signifies this need for something to be publicly recognised. We are perhaps acknowledging also that we have undersold ourselves and need to sell ourselves better in order to achieve the goal for which we are aiming.

Advice

Inner awareness often manifests itself as a figure which is giving advice. The wise old man or woman is an archetypal representation of the part of us that knows what we should be doing. Receiving advice from someone may highlight a need to listen to others.

Aeroplane

An aeroplane suggests a swift easy journey with some attention to detail necessary. Interestingly, the aeroplane can symbolise both a new sexual relationship as well as a new awareness of spiritual matters. An airport signifies a state of transition and an airman or pilot is either a romanticised picture of the Animus or of the Self, that part of ourselves which will 'get us there'.

Affair

We need to come to terms with our own sexual needs and desires for excitement and stimulation. Dreaming of an affair allows us to release such feelings. We may feel the need to do something naughty or to take emotional risks.

Such a dream may also indicate the need to integrate a perhaps unrecognised part of ourselves or to learn to love that part of us represented by the lover.

Alcohol – *see* **Intoxication** *and* **Wine**

Alien
Dreaming of aliens usually suggests that we are in touch with a part of
ourselves which is unknown and frightening, and which needs to be
faced. There is the potential for experiencing oneself – or a part of
oneself – as not belonging.

There are increasing numbers of people who dream of being abducted
by aliens. Often these dreams contain an element where the physical
body is being explored or changed in some way, often from a sexual
point of view. Many women believe they have become pregnant because
of this, and thus do in fact become different from other people. Whether
this is some kind of hysterical reaction, a genuine step on the path of self-
development, or is in fact real is difficult to evaluate. Most alien figures
do seem to have certain characteristics in common, and may be linking
with an archetypal impression.

Alone
Being single, isolated or lonely in dreams can suggest issues to do with
independence. Loneliness can be experienced as a negative state, whereas
being alone can be positive. In dreams a feeling can be particularly
highlighted in order for us to recognise whether it is positive or negative,
and whether we can deal with our own emotional make-up without the
help of others. Often being alone in a dream suggests that there is a
wholeness or completeness about us which indicates a degree of self-
sufficiency.

Altar – *see also* **Religious Imagery** *and* **Table**
Almost inevitably there is some religious significance in dreaming of an
altar. Since pagan times an altar has represented the surface from which
a sacrifice, or act of making sacred, of some sort is made and thus an altar
can also signify a dedication to a cause or objective. An altar thus
becomes a symbol of the public acknowledgement of one's efforts or
beliefs. In more esoteric terms an altar represents the meeting of the
physical and spiritual realms, and the communion or coming together of
like-minded people.

Amputation

Amputation in dreams suggests some kind of loss of power or ability, or some disfigurement of the perfection of each individual. When we speak of something costing an arm or a leg we are aware that the price of something is exorbitant, and this type of imagery can pop up in dreams. Giving away our power or integrity may be too great a price to pay within a particular situation in our lives. To dream of amputating someone else's limb indicates our ability to deny others their right to self-expression. Many sayings evolve from acts to do with amputation, e.g. 'I'd give my right arm for that'.

Anaesthetic

Trying to avoid painful emotions, and feeling overpowered by external circumstances can lead to dreams of being anaesthetised. It may be that we are trying, or being forced, to avoid something that we cannot or do not want to face. We would rather cut the situation off painfully than face the consequences. Occasionally such a dream will indicate the need to be quiescent and let events unfold around us.

Ancestors

Our conformity, ways of behaving, ethics and our religious observances are all handed down from generation to generation. When we become conscious of our ancestors in a dream we are focusing on our roots, and perhaps questioning them. We may begin to understand of ourselves through our relationship with the past, either our own or others'.

Anchor

The necessity to remain stable in emotional situations often means that we need to catch hold of a concept or idea which will give us a point of reference in difficult situations. We have to become grounded in order to weather the storm. Occasionally an anchor can suggest a spiritual concept which represents hope and sanctuary.

Antlers – *see also* **Horns**

Traditionally supernatural powers, fertility and nobleness of spirit are represented by antlers. More mundanely, antlers will suggest masculine supremacy and power, intellectual or otherwise. In many supposedly more primitive societies powdered antler horn enhanced sexual prowess, or gave one the power of the animal concerned.

Anvil

The anvil is an image which belongs to the mists of time , and will probably therefore not come to consciousness, unless perhaps one is learning about basic forces, or studying mythology. It contains within the symbolism the idea of creating a spark, and therefore new life, or of tempering a basic energy into something useable and more highly polished.

Apron

The apron is such a symbol of domesticity that its original function as a protective garment or even a badge of office as in Freemasonry has largely been lost. In many cases dreaming of an apron suggests ties with one's mother or the more nurturing side of the personality.

Appointment

Normally in dreams time has a strange way of lengthening or shortening according to the demands of the particular scenario. Therefore to be aware of an actual appointment in a dream, such as going to the dentist or a solicitor, suggests having an aim or objective in mind, perhaps to do with acting professionally or appropriately.

Arch

Passing through an arch or doorway in dreams usually indicates some kind of initiation or rite of passage. We move into a new phase of life, perhaps taking on new responsibilities, learning new skills and meeting new people. There may be some kind of test, but the way is not barred to us: we are simply required to make the effort.

Arena

An arena suggests a ritualised conflict. Today sport is used as a release from tension. By creating an environment where conflict can be dealt with we allow more space for self-expression and creativity. Old style arenas were often circular and tiered to preserve a hierarchical system.

Armour

Armour in dreams signifies chivalry, protection and the need to protect or be protected, possibly from something we feel is threatening us. It may be that there is a degree of old fashioned rigidity in our make-up which prevents us from moving into new situations.

Arms – *see also* Body

Arms – in the sense of weapons – are used to protect and defend. There was quite a series of rituals to do with the Page becoming the Knight and making the transition from the arms bearer to the user. In dreams arms may suggest that we are defending ourselves, fighting, being held or acknowledging.

Arrow

Arrows as weapons suggest power, energy and expertise – they can also symbolise words in dreams. We could either hurt or be hurt by directness, and there is the need to be aware of the consequences of our actions.

In today's world of signs and symbolism the arrow can indicate the direction our lives should take.

Asceticism

To meet an ascetic or holy man in a dream is to meet our higher self, and to recognise the part of ourselves which is continually seeking union with the ultimate or whatever our idea of the divine is. There may be conflict with natural drives, such as a search for celibacy. We are looking for clarity and purpose.

Ashes

When a situation has outlived its usefulness and there is nothing more to be learnt we may dream of ashes. When a relationship ends, ashes whether dead or hot can indicate sorrow. These are what remains of our experience which will enable us to make the best of a situation.

Attack

The interpretation of the dream will depend on whether the dreamer is being attacked or is the aggressor. Being attacked in a dream indicates a fear of being under threat from external events or internal emotions. Impulses or ideas which the dreamer does not fully understand force the dreamer into taking a defensive position. If the dreamer is the attacker he needs a more positive form of self-expression.

Aura
The aura is an energy field which surrounds the physical body. It is a representation of the power we hold within, the force field with which we repel and attract people. It is an expression of the Self-, particularly if we are undergoing a period of self-improvement. Perceiving an aura in a dream indicates how powerful we consider ourselves – or others – to be.

Authority Figures (such as judges, police, teachers etc.)
Our impression of authority is first developed through our relationship with our father or father figure. Often depending on how we were treated as children, our view of authority will be anything from a benign helper to an exploitative disciplinarian. Most authority figures will ultimately lead us back to what is right for us, although not necessarily what we might consider good. Authority figures in dreams initially appear to have power over us, though if worked with properly will generate the power to succeed, and may come to be viewed in terms of the Higher Self. Dreaming particularly of police can indicate a kind of social control and a protective element for us as members of society. Often a policeman will appear in dreams as one's conscience. We may feel that our wilder, more renegade side needs controlling.

Avalanche
Psychologically, we need to regain control of forces either within or outside ourselves. The power of frozen emotions could overwhelm us and we may therefore be in danger.

Axe
Esoterically, the axe represents power; thunder; conquest of error and sacrifice. So in dreams we become aware of the destructive force which may be needed to take us out of a particular situation. The axe is often also a symbol of time.

B

Baby

To dream about a baby that is our own, indicates that we need to recognise those vulnerable feelings over which we have no control. We may be attempting a new project or way of life which is literally 'our baby'. Dreaming of a foetus rather than a fully-formed baby suggests that the project or idea has not yet been properly formed sufficient for it to survive on its own. If the baby is someone else's in the dream we need to be aware of that person's vulnerability, and to recognise that we cannot interfere in a certain situation, or that they may be innocent of something. Psychologically we are in touch with the innocent, curious side of ourselves, with the part which neither wants nor needs responsibility. Dreaming of a baby can indicate that, on a spiritual level, the dreamer has a need for a feeling of purity.

Back/Backbone – *see also* Body

If the backbone is particularly noticeable in the dream we need to consider our main support structure, and also either our firmness of character or perhaps some rigidity in our personality. Someone else's back may suggest that they are not giving us sufficient support, though it may also signify that a particular situation no longer has a place in our lives.

Backwards

Regressive tendencies can cause us to move backwards into previous behaviour patterns. To dream of going backwards indicates that we may be slow to learn, and should withdraw gracefully from a situation. Continuing with a course of action may be detrimental and impede our progress.

Badge

Dreaming of a badge shows our need to be accepted not just as ourselves, but also as part of a greater whole, and to belong to a group of special people while still maintaining our own identity. We are aware that certain qualities in ourselves need to be recognised and the wearing of a badge is showing the world those qualities.

Bag

The dreamer may be having problems with the feminine or more secret elements in his or her identity. Everybody needs a certain amount of privacy, and a bag allows us to carry around our emotions in public without openly displaying them. Any container tends to signify the more feminine attributes and therefore, by association, intuition and hidden meanings.

Baggage

An indication of the dreamer's feelings of sorrow can manifest in dreams as baggage. The dreamer is under some psychological stress, carrying past hurt or trauma, and may be carrying an extra load, either emotional or practical.

Bait

There is an aspect of our lives which needs to be enticed out into the open. In a woman's dream putting down bait can be an indication of her doubts about her own ability to attract a partner. The bait could be an action or the use of a particular emotion in order to achieve the end result.

Baker

This old-fashioned figure symbolises nurture and caring, and our ability to change our circumstances by our own means.

Balance

In dreams balance and all symbols associated with balance are to do with maintaining one's equilibrium in the face of difficulty. The circumstances we find ourselves in will demonstrate what the difficulty may be and show us how we need to weigh things up in order to act appropriately.

To be looking at financial balances or at balancing the books generally means a consideration of the resources we have available to us.

Balcony

Psychologically we are searching for power within a situation in which we feel powerless. To dream of being on a balcony indicates that we are searching for a higher status than we have at present, or are aware of the fact that within a particular situation we have a degree of competence and wisdom. A balcony indicates both support and protectiveness. It can also represent the Mother in her protective aspect.

Ball

A ball connects with the playful, childlike side of ourselves and our need to express ourselves with freedom. In dreams the sphere also suggests perfection and completeness, that is both structure and freedom. Solar and lunar festivals are symbolised by games with balls, when there is much laughter and fun. This of course then leads us to the ball in the sense of a formal party, again allowing us to mark a special occasion, or rite of passage.

Ballerina – *see also* Dance

We are aware of the creative side of ourselves, and the need for controlled movement through music, grace and the inner aspect of Feeling. Also we are searching for balance and poise.

Balloon

A balloon is a symbol for joy, and in dreams it may introduce a note of fun amid seriousness. It may often make us aware of our 'humanness' but also our search for the spiritual, or more free-spirited side of our personalities, often a feeling of 'light-spirited' joy, or indeed the spirit rising.

Very often it is the colour of balloons in our dreams which is important (*see* **Colours**).

Ban

To be excluded from anything is perhaps one of man's biggest fears, since this ties in with a basic feeling of rejection. To be banned from a favourite place in dreams suggests that we have not come up to scratch in some way, or are not conforming with authority. Banning someone ourselves signifies that we do not approve of an action or feeling.

Band

Some kind of band or tape suggests that the dreamer is marking (or needs to mark) some kind of limitation within his life. Perhaps there is a restriction or exclusion operating, which needs to be acknowledged.

A musical band or group in dreams indicates the basic harmony which can exist in each of us, but could also suggest the type of behaviour to which we aspire – maybe recognition for talent, or suitable remuneration for our efforts.

Bandage

Bandages signify preservation or a protective healing process. There may be hurt feelings or emotional injuries which need attention. If a bandage is being applied in a dream this shows the beginning of a healing process, which may be self-motivated. If it is being taken off the healing process is over, and we are free of restriction.

Bank

A bank indicates a secure spiritual space, from which we can manage whatever resources we have. Those resources may be material, emotional, mental or spiritual. For many, a bank will suggest resources held in reserve for uses as we need them.

A river bank would suggest the boundary between our emotional and practical selves.

Our financial, mental or spiritual resources may need careful management.

Banner – *see also* Flag

A banner appearing in a dream can stand for some kind of ideal which may, for instance, be a certain standard of acceptable behaviour. An old fashioned banner – as used in medieval battles – indicates a need to consolidate thoughts and actions as a group, and perhaps agree on a particular course of action. Such a crusade may require some statement of commitment.

Baptism – *see also* Religious Imagery

Baptism is a rite of passage, and as such is symbolic of many things –

initiation; death and rebirth; regeneration; renewal. The basic link of all these is the feeling of optimism that it brings. The dreamer is probably aware of moving into a new phase of existence, perhaps having made a promise or vow along the way.

Bar – *see also* **Public House**

The bar is a symbol of our spiritual power, and power in everyday life. We need to handle ourselves with strength of purpose, but when we dream of a bar, such as an iron bar, we should look at how rigid or aggressive we are being in our behaviour.

A bar, in the sense of a public house, can represent masculinity or perhaps behaviour which is designed to give us relaxation and fun. This will depend of course on the dreamer's conscious beliefs about such places.

To stand at a bar may represent a barrier to our sexual enjoyment, particularly in the male.

Barefoot

Being barefoot at one time indicated great humility. When Christ wished to show that he was no different from other men he washed his disciples' feet. Depending on the circumstances of the dream, to be barefoot can indicate either poverty, humility or the recognition of sensual freedom. A common dream is to have lost one's shoes, which has a great deal to do with appropriate behaviour.

Basket

An old style interpretation of a dream of a basket full of bread suggests nurturing and sharing – as in a sacramental meal. By association a basket therefore represents the feminine, nurturing, fruition and abundance.

Bath/Bathing

To dream of bathing someone shows the need to nurture or to have an intimate connection with that person. When we dream of being in the bath, it may indicate the need for cleansing of some old feelings, the need to relax, to let go. We have an opportunity to contemplate what has occurred in the past and to adopt new attitudes.

Interestingly ritual bathing and cleansing is said to enhance the ability to dream.

Bay

To dream of a seashore and be conscious of a bay or inlet is said to show we are aware of a woman's sexuality and receptiveness. The wolf baying at the moon shows the overcoming of basic animal instincts. To be keeping something at bay indicates a need to be on our guard.

Beach

The sea usually suggests emotion, so in dreams to be on a beach shows our awareness of the boundary between emotion and reality, our ability to be in touch with the elements. Depending on our actions and state of mind in the dream, dreaming of a beach usually means relaxation and creativity.

Beacon

Beacons in dreams may light the way to spiritual enlightenment and spiritual sanctuary. They can show, variously, a warning, the need for communication or a strongly held principle by which one lives.

Bean

To be storing beans, which in ancient folklore signify immortality and magic power, in a dream may show a fear of failure, or lack of confidence in our ability to carry through a mission, or the need to create something in the future. To be planting beans would suggest faith in the future, and a wish to create something useful. Traditionally the bean was supposed to be capable of feeding, clothing and providing an object of exchange for barter.

Bear

The mother appears in dreams in many guises, the bear among them. The image may be of the possessive, devouring mother or of the all-caring mother. If it is recognised in the dream that the bear is masculine the image may then be of an overbearing person, or possibly the father.

Beard

Spiritually there are two meanings in interpreting the symbol of the beard and the meaning will depend on the culture. It may mean wisdom and dignity, or it may mean deceit and deviousness. To dream of a man with a beard means we must guard against cover-up and deceit. We also need to consider more masculine attributes in ourselves or others.

Beating

If in dreams one is taking a beating, humility, anguish and grief are symbolised. To be beaten either physically or in a game indicates submission on our part to a greater force. The act of beating something or someone represents our need for 'power over' by our aggression and brute force, and possibly an anger in us which cannot be expressed properly in waking life.

Bed

A bed can represent a form of spiritual sanctuary and a sense of purity. To be going to bed alone in a dream can indicate a desire for a return to the safety and security of the womb. To dream of a bed made up with fresh linen indicates the need for a fresh approach to those thoughts and ideas that really matter to us.

Bee/Beehive

The bee symbolises immortality, rebirth and order. As something to be feared, as well as trained and used, the meaning of bees in dreams can be ambivalent. Folk tales, such as the one about telling one's troubles to the bees, can surface in dreams without us necessarily recognising what they mean. The beehive is said to represent an ordered community and therefore the ability to absorb chaos.

To be stung by a bee is a warning of the possibility of hurt, but can also suggest penetration. Being attacked by a swarm indicates we are creating a situation which may become uncontrollable. To dream of tending a beehive alerts us to the need for good management of our resources, and an awareness of the need for hard work.

Beetle – *see also* **Insects**

The scarab beetle in Egyptian mythology represents protection from evil, and its ability to cleanse an environment represents hard work. Thought by many to be dirty, in a dream the beetle carries the same symbolism as all insects – that is, something which is unclean or not properly attended to.

Bell

Traditionally, to hear a bell tolling in a dream was to be warned of disaster or of a death. Bells can also indicate the conscience, and our need to seek approval from others. By forewarning us of risk or danger they alert us to potential mistakes. Dreaming of a bell, such as a door bell, may indicate that we have a desire to communicate with someone.

Belt

A belt may be an insignia of power particularly if it seems ornate in the dream. Additionally we may be 'hide-bound' through outdated material, attitudes and duty.

Bicycle

As a representation of duality the bicycle epitomises youth and freedom. A bicycle can also denote effort which needs to be made to succeed. We should pay particular attention to our personal effort and motivation.

Birth

We tend to dream of birth at the beginning of a new way of life, a new attitude, new ability, or a new project – also when we become aware of the death of the old.

Blindfolding

In spiritual terms, blindfolding is a rite of passage. It is a transition between two states. If we are conscious in a dream of a blindfold there may be something we are deliberately not seeing or being shown (this ties in with the interpretation of blindness).

Blindness

Spiritually, blindness is a form of ignorance. It can suggest the irrational. It is also a form of initiation as in the blindness of St. Paul on the road to Damascus. In dreams it may be that we are choosing not to use knowledge appropriately.

Boats – *see also* **Sailing**

It will depend on what kind of boat is depicted. A small rowing boat would suggest an emotional journey, which requires a great deal of effort; a yacht might suggest a similar journey done with style; whereas a large ship would suggest creating new horizons but in the company of others. A speedboat might represent an adventurous spirit, a canoe a different personally challenging way of working.

What happens to the boat in the dream will have relevance as a reflection of our waking life. Running aground, pulling into harbour and so on are easily interpreted. Disembarking shows the end of a project or period, successful or otherwise. Making a long sea voyage suggests leaving friends and family, as would running away to sea. If we miss the boat we have not paid enough attention to detail in a project in our waking lives, or we do not have enough information. Any narrow waterway or river signifies the birth experience. A ship usually represents the feminine because of its capriciousness. A ferry holds all the symbolism of the journey across the River Styx after death. It is the giving up of selfish desires. After this we may be 'reborn' into a better life, or way of life. It may also represent a transition in our lives.

Body

The body in dreams signifies the individual and all that he is. In dreams, the body often represents the Ego. The body forms the prime source of information about ourselves, and often highlights problems we may have on a physical level. Those aware of other systems of belief will often find knowledge fed to them through dreams about the body. Psychologically, most of what happens to us is translated into feeling about the body, and therefore becomes a fertile source of symbolism in dreams. When emotions cannot be faced in ordinary everyday life, they very often become distorted dream symbols.

Different aspects of the body can have various meanings in dreams. For example, to dream of the upper part of the body is to link with the intellect and the spiritual aspects of the character, while the lower part of the body represents the inborn emotional aspects of a character. An adult's head on an immature body, or a child's head on an adult body, is an indication that the dreamer needs to recognise the difference between mature thought and emotion. If there is conflict between the upper and lower part it indicates that there is disharmony between the mental faculties and instinctive behaviour. The right side or hand being especially noticeable in dreams signifies we should take note of the logical side of our personality, whereas the left side or left hand indicates we need to be aware of our intuitive, creative side.

Body parts can have relevance as follows:

Abdomen, stomach, belly When the dream concentrates on the abdomen, there is a need to focus on emotions and repressed feelings.

Anus – *see also* **Excrement** In dreams, the mind returns to the initial gaining of the control of bodily functions, as evidence of self-realisation, self-reliance and control but also of suppression and defence. Such a dream therefore is indicating an aspect of childish behaviour or egotism.

Arms We use our arms in all sorts of different ways. In dreams we may be defending ourselves, fighting or being held. We may also be showing passionate commitment.

Back Dreaming of seeing someone else's back suggests we should identify the more private elements in our own personality. Other people may not at this present time wish to share their thoughts with us, or indeed may suggest contempt or disapproval. We may also be exposed to the unexpected happening. If we dream of turning our backs we are rejecting the particular feeling being experienced in the dream.

Backbone If the backbone is particularly noticeable in a dream, we should consider the main support structure in our lives. Intellectually, we need to consider our firmness of character.

Becoming fat or thin To dream of a change in body shape suggests change in our personality or in the way we handle trauma.

Blood Many people fear blood, and thus a dream about blood can highlight the need to handle such fears. On a more spiritual level it represents the blood of Christ or martyrdom, and that a sacrifice is being made. This links into the ancient belief that the blood contained the life of the spirit, and therefore spilt blood was sacred. It can also represent renewal of life through its connection with menstruation.

Breasts Usually, breasts in dreams indicate our connection with the mother figure and our need for nurturing. Such a dream can also depict a wish to return to being an infant without responsibilities.

Constipation (in life as well as in dreams) Withholding signifies an inability to let go of the past or of previous patterns of behaviour, and an inability to perform adequately.

Excrement The dreamer may not have gone beyond the feeling that anything to do with bodily functions is dirty and self-centred. There may be an element of rebellion in the dreamer's waking life. Playing with excrement can also represent money and value, so in a dream this can highlight an anxiety about money, as well as, possibly, a fear of responsibility.

If the excrement is transformed into living animals, maybe rats, the dreamer is coming to terms with the fact that he is responsible for managing his own impulses. Excrement in its more spiritual meaning belongs to the realm of feelings and we may simply be trying to get rid of bad feelings. Those bad feelings can be turned into something worthwhile. Evacuation of the bowel usually highlights our need to be free of worry and responsibility, or possibly the need to learn how to be uninhibited. It can also in dreams signify the sexual act.

Eye Any dream to do with the eye is to do with observation and discrimination. It has a connection with the power of light and, in ancient times, of the sun gods. Through its connection with Egyptian symbolism, the eye is also a talisman. Loss of eyesight suggests loss of clarity, and depending on which eye can be either the loss of logic (right eye) or loss of intuition (left eye). Regaining the eyesight can indicate a return to the innocence and clear-sightedness of the child.

Hair The hair represents strength and virility. In dreams, to be combing the hair is to be attempting to untangle a particular attitude we may have. To be having our hair cut is to be trying to create order in our lives. To be cutting someone else's hair may be to be curtailing an activity (It is possible that there may be some fear or doubt connected with sexuality). To be bald in a dream is to recognise one's own intelligence or wisdom.

Hand The hands are two of the most expressive parts of the body and signify power and creativity. The two hands contrasted with each other, a different object in each hand show there may be some conflict in the dreamer between his belief and his feelings. A hand on the breast signifies submission. Clasped hands indicate union or friendship, while clenched hands suggest a threat. Folded hands suggest deep repose, or a state of rest. The hands covering the eyes generally represent shame or horror, while hands crossed at the wrists suggest that one is being bound. The open hand represents justice, and the laying-on of hands signifies healing and blessing (particularly if the hand is placed on the neck). The hands placed together signify defencelessness, while placed in someone else's are an indication of a kind of surrender. When the hands are raised this can indicate either adoration, prayer or surrender; if the palms are turned outwards a blessing is being given, while when they are raised to the head the dreamer should give a great deal of thought and care to his situation. Washing the hands suggests innocence or rejection of guilt, while wringing the hands signifies grief and distress. A huge hand, particularly from the sky, suggests that one has been 'specially chosen'. The right hand is the 'power' hand, while the left is passive and receptive. Sometimes in dreams the left hand can represent cheating.

According to ancient belief which is now again in vogue, each finger suggests a certain quality: first finger – expansion, second finger – restriction, third finger – the self and little finger – communication. Thus a pointing finger can suggest a way forward or a special kind of selection.

Head The head is the principal part of the body. Because it is the seat of intellect, it denotes power and wisdom. Dreaming of the head suggests that we should look very carefully at the way we deal with both intelligence and folly. To dream of the head being bowed suggests prayer or invocation. When the head is covered we may be covering up our own intelligence or acknowledging somebody else's superiority. A blow to the head in a dream can indicate that we should reconsider our actions in a particular situation.

Heart The heart is the centre of the being and represents 'feeling' wisdom rather than intellectual wisdom. It is also representative of compassion, understanding and love.

Heel This suggests the part of ourselves which is strong but, at the same time, vulnerable.

Jaw The jaw depicts our way of expressing ourselves. Spiritually, it is also thought to signify the opening to the underworld.

Kidneys The kidneys are organs of elimination; therefore to dream of them is to be aware of the need for cleansing.

Knees The knees are symbolic of prayer and entreaty, and of emotional commitment.

Limbs In dreams any limb can be taken to mean sexuality and fears associated with gender issues. Being dismembered can be taken in its literal sense – we are being torn apart. Sometimes this can suggest the need to restructure our lives and begin again. At other times it can indicate that there is a way in which we are being threatened to the very core of our existence.

Liver The liver is representative of irritability and suppressed anger.

Lungs In Chinese medicine the lungs represent grief. They are also involved in decision making. Spiritually, the lungs are the seat of righteousness, and the source of thoughts concerning the Self. Highlighted in dreams, they can represent the breath of life.

Mouth The mouth represents the devouring, demanding part of ourselves, and by implication the feminine, receptive side. The circumstances of the dream may give a clue to the correct interpretation.

Nose The nose in dreams can stand for curiosity, and also for intuition. Sometimes it is also representative of the penis.

Penis Dreaming of a penis – either one's own or someone else's – usually highlights the attitude to penetrative sex.

Skin Skin in a dream stands for our persona, or the protective camouflage we create for others.

Teeth Teeth are said to stand for aggressive sexuality. Teeth falling or coming out easily means we are going through some form of transition, e.g. from childhood to maturity, or from maturity to old age and helplessness. If one is anxious about teeth dropping out it suggests there is a fear of getting old and undesirable, or an anxiety about maturing. In a woman's dream, if the teeth are swallowed this can signify pregnancy.

Throat Dreaming of the throat denotes awareness of our vulnerability and also of the need for self-expression.

Thumb Dreaming of a thumb suggests awareness of how powerful we are. The thumb pointing upwards represents beneficial energy, but pointing downwards is negative. This latter was used as the death signal for Roman gladiators.

Tongue The tongue in dreams may be associated with our understanding of information that we wish to pass on to other people. We may have deeply felt beliefs we wish to share, but need to know when to speak and when to remain silent. Another explanation that is much more basic is that of the symbolism of the serpent and the phallus, and hence sexuality.

Urine Urine in a dream often indicates our feelings about emotional control. We may either yield to emotion or bottle it up. How we deal with urine often also tells us a great deal about our own sexuality.

Vagina Most often, dreams of the vagina are to do with one's self-image. In a woman's dream, it highlights her receptivity. In a man's dream it suggests his need to be penetrative, both mentally and physically.

Womb The womb represents a return to the beginning. We all have need of security and shelter, and freedom from responsibility. Dreams of the womb can signify our need to satisfy those requirements. On a slightly more esoteric level, the womb represents our connection with the Great Mother or Mother Earth. Dreams of returning to the womb suggest a reconnection with the passive, more yielding side of our nature. We may need a period of self-healing and recuperation.

Bomb

In dreams bombs appearing suggest that our own emotions are likely to get the better of us. We may be in some kind of explosive situation with which we need to deal. A bomb actually exploding is usually an unexpected event. Dreaming of such an explosion would suggest a fear of sudden death.

Book – *see also* Reading

Our search for knowledge and the ability to learn from other people's experience is symbolised in dreams by books and libraries. To dream of old books represents inherited wisdom and spiritual awareness. To dream of sacred books, such as the Bible or Koran, signify hidden or sacred knowledge. To dream of more practical books, such as account books indicates the need or ability to look after our own resources.

Border

To have our attention drawn to the edge or border of material often indicates changes we will make in the material world. To be standing on a border between two countries would show the need to be making great changes in life; perhaps physically moving our place of residence or making decisive changes in the way we think and feel. Meeting new experiences may give us the sense of crossing a barrier or border.

Bottle
To a certain extent it depends on which type of bottle is perceived in the dream. To see a baby's feeding bottle would indicate the need to be successfully nurtured and helped to grow. A bottle of alcohol would show the need to celebrate, or to curb an excess, while a medicine bottle might symbolise the need to look at one's own health. A broken bottle could indicate either aggression or failure.

Boy
To have a dream about a boy shows the potential for development through new experience. If the boy is known he reflects aspects of the dreamer's personality which he or she is learning to understand. Emotionally, we may need to be in touch with ourselves at that age and with the unsophisticated naiveté and passion that a boy has. We are contacting our natural drives and ability to face difficulties.

Boyfriend
To dream of a boyfriend, whether present or former, associates with the feelings, attachments and sexuality connected with him, and our concept of how he expresses himself. To dream of having as a boyfriend someone whom you would not anticipate, e.g. someone you do not like, indicates the need to have a greater understanding of the way you relate to men, and particularly that type of individual. Consideration may need to be given to the loving, nurturing side of masculinity.

Bow
Since bowing is indicative of giving someone else status, to be bowing to someone in a dream would indicate our sense of inferiority. To perceive a bow, as in Cupid's bow, within a dream can indicate the need to be loved – the union of masculine and feminine. To see a bow made of ribbon in a dream is making a connection to the feminine principle and to beauty – it may also represent some form of celebration.

Bowl

The bowl is one of the oldest dream symbols known. A bowl of water represents the feminine, fertility and the receptive principle or our capacity for emotion. A bowl of food in a dream represents our ability to nurture and sustain others. A bowl of flowers can represent a gift or a talent.

Box

Various types of boxes perceived in a dream may represent different aspects of the feminine personality. This arises from the old symbol of the square representing the physical aspect of the feminine.

To feel boxed in in a dream is to be prevented from expanding in an appropriate way, while to dream of packing things in a box suggests that we are not able to deal with feelings or thoughts which are giving us difficulty.

Break

To dream of something being broken symbolises loss or damage. If the dreamer actually dreams of breaking something, appropriate action needs to be taken in order to break a bond or connection in the dreamer's life. If a favourite object is broken we must make changes and break from the past or give up a cherished principle.

Bridge

A bridge in a dream signifies the emotional connection between the dreamer and other people or various parts and aspects of his life. It is one of the most commonly found images in dreams and almost invariably indicates the crossing from one phase of life to another, some kind of rite of passage, and for this reason it can sometimes indicate death. The bridge may be depicted as weak or strong, sturdy or otherwise, which gives an indication of the strength of connection necessary to make changes in the dreamer's life.

Bridle

Symbolically a degree of spiritual restraint or control is often needed. To be bridled in a dream, as in being yoked to something, indicates the need for focused effort. If the bridle is made of flowers it indicates a more feminine way of imposing control. If the bridle is harsher – such as one of metal and/or leather – we perhaps need to be harder on ourselves or on someone we love.

Brutality

Brutality manifests itself in demonic acts of evil. Unrestrained passion – whether sexual or otherwise – can appear as brutality and cruelty in our dreams. To experience some form of brutality in a dream can be frightening until we realise that we are connecting into the darker, more animal side of ourselves. We may need to deal with fears associated with that side of ourselves.

Bubble

Bubbles as beautiful but fragile objects remind us of the transitory nature of human existence, that nothing is permanent. We may dream of bubbles as part of our need to have fun in a childlike way. We often become aware of the temporary nature of happiness, and our need for illusion. A bubble represents the illusory elements of everyday life and, more specifically, the day dreams.

Buckle

A buckle can have a double meaning in this case. It can represent a protective element against the forces of evil; it can also help us take the strain and not 'buckle' under pressure. To be fastening a buckle in a dream shows that we accept responsibility for what we do.

Burial – *see also* Death

To have a dream about being buried either alive or dead indicates a fear of being overcome, possibly by responsibility, or of repressing parts of our personality in ways which are harmful. To be attending a burial in our dreams shows the need to come to terms with loss, particularly of something that we value.

The obvious spiritual symbols of death, loss and pain are also relevant here. This is not necessarily a negative meaning, it can also be positive; the dreamer should look at the resurrection and the positive elements that it can bring.

Bus

A bus journey is that part of our lives where we are aware of the need to be on the move, but particularly to be with other people, with whom we have a common aim. Such a journey has a great deal to do with our public image. Trouble with timetables, e.g. missing the bus, arriving too early or missing a connection denotes that we are having difficulty with our external lives and perhaps should re-evaluate how we want to live our lives. Getting on the wrong bus or going the wrong way means that there are conflicting needs and desires and we need to be aware of our own inner intuition. This is usually a warning of a wrong action. Dreaming of not being able to pay the fare shows that we do not have enough resources to set out on a particular course of action.

Butterfly

When seen in dreams or meditation, the butterfly represents the freed soul and immortality. There is no need for the soul to be trapped by the physical body, although psychologically the butterfly can indicate a lack of ability to settle down or to undertake a protracted task. On a practical level, when seen in dreams, the butterfly represents light-heartedness and freedom.

Cage/Cell – *see also* **Prison**

The cage normally represents some form of trap or jail. To dream of caging a wild animal alerts us to our need to restrain our wilder instincts. To dream that we are in a cage indicates a sense of frustration and perhaps of being trapped by the past.

We are being warned that we are enforcing too much restraint on our hidden abilities and not using them correctly. We could be allowing others to hold us back in some way.

Calendar

Time is a self-imposed limitation, so when anything that marks time appears in a dream we are being warned of the potential for limitation. Our attention may be being drawn to the past, present or future and something significant in our lives.

Camera

To be using a camera in a dream means we are recording events or occasions which we may need to remember or take note of more fully. Being filmed indicates that we need to look more carefully at our actions and reactions to certain situations.

Cancer

To dream of a cancer, one of our most primal fears, indicates that we are out of harmony with our body. It indicates fear of illness and equally can represent something 'eating away' at us – usually a negative idea or concept. Intellectually we may have worked through our fears but still be left with attitudes and beliefs that cannot be cleared away, and very often this appears as cancer in dreams.

There is also the astrological sign of Cancer to bear in mind – The Mother and The Moon.

Candle

To dream of candles indicates that we are trying to clarify something that we do not understand. Candles on a birthday cake can therefore indicate that we are marking a transition from the old to the new. Lighting a candle represents using courage and fortitude or asking for something that we need. Psychologically candles can represent knowledge or wisdom that has not fully crystallised. They can also represent our control of personal magic. On another level candles suggest illumination, wisdom, strength and beauty.

Cannibalism

Cannibalism in dreams represents inappropriate behaviour. To be aware of eating human flesh may indicate our dislike of unsuitable foods or actions. There is often a part of ourselves we have not 'internalised' which we need to absorb. Eating human flesh in a dream can mean that we are taking in wrong information. It also symbolises the absorption of powers or qualities belonging to someone else.

Canoe

To dream of a canoe indicates that we are handling our emotions in isolation though we are possibly making efforts to control the flow of our emotion. We are aware that we are capable of making changes but only by our own efforts. We may be protected from our emotions, but may also be at risk.

Canopy

Dreaming of a canopy suggests that we need protection, shelter or love – or possibly all three. As a canopy protects the head – the seat of intellect – we may have a need to draw attention to higher ideals or aspirations.

Car

The car is representative of our own personal space. To dream of being in a car usually alerts us to our own motivation. Therefore, driving the car can indicate our need to achieve a goal, while being a passenger could indicate that we have handed over responsibility for our lives to someone else. Dream scenarios involving cars are often more to do with what we are doing to ourselves on a psychological or emotional level. Being alone in a vehicle indicates independence, while dreaming of the brakes of a car shows one's ability to be in control of a situation.

The car engine indicates the essential drives with which we have to deal. A crashing vehicle suggests fear of failure in life, while a car on fire denotes stress of some sort, either physical or emotional.

To be in a car which is driven carelessly, either by the dreamer or someone else, marks a lack of responsibility, while a feeling of being left behind would be shown by your car being overtaken. To dream of reversing a car registers a feeling that one is slipping backwards or having to reverse a decision.

Cards (Greeting)
To dream of giving or receiving a card such as a birthday card alerts us to the need for a specific kind of communication with the addressee. Our subconscious may be registering concern, either about ourselves or others. On another level, there may be a need for visual communication, that is, the ability to convey a message spiritually.

Cards (Playing)
In a dream, playing cards highlights our ability to be open to opportunity or to take chances. The cards that one deals, or is dealt, in a dream may have significance as to number or as to suit. Hearts indicate emotion and relationship. Diamonds represent material wealth. Spades represent conflict, difficulties and obstacles. Clubs represent action, work and intelligence. The King portrays human success and mastery. The Queen indicates emotional depth, sensitivity and understanding. The Jack represents impetuousness, creativity or an adolescent energy.

Carriage
Dreaming of a carriage, such as a horse drawn one, could be suggestive of old fashioned attitudes to modern thinking. A train carriage would indicate that we are taking a journey that is slightly more public in character than a car journey. Any symbol that signifies our being moved in some way usually draws attention to our ability to make progressive changes in our lives. The carriage is also a symbol of majesty and power.

Carried/Carrying

To be aware of carrying an object suggests we need to look at what is being accepted as a burden or difficulty. If we dream of being carried we may feel that we are in need of support. To dream of carrying someone registers the fact that we may be accepting responsibility for someone else and that this responsibility is a burden.

Cat

To dream of cats is to link with the sensuous side in human beings, usually in women. The refined, but also the powerful, yet self-reliant aspect of woman may also be suggested by the cat. Goddesses such as Bast the Egyptian cat goddess are usually represented as having two sides to their natures, one devious and one helpful, so the cat often denotes the capricious side of the feminine.

Cauldron – *see also* Kettle

The cauldron symbolises abundance, sustenance and nourishment. The magic cauldron represents feminine power and fertility. On another level, it may be that we need to acknowledge our intuitive abilities.

Cave

A cave represents a doorway into the unconscious. While initially the cave may be frightening, an exploration can reveal strong contact with our own inner selves. Passing through the cave signifies a change of state, and a deeper understanding of our own negative impulses.

Cemetery

A cemetery in a dream can mean both the part of ourselves that we have no use for and also our thoughts and feelings about death. Both things need to be handled, though the latter also entails dealing with the fear we may have surrounding death.

Centre

To dream of being at the centre of something highlights our awareness of our ability to be powerful within a situation; that everything revolves around us. To be moving away from the centre indicates that part of our lives may be off balance. Psychologically, to be at the centre or in the middle of a situation we need to be aware of both our ability to control that situation and our ability to be flexible. Moving towards the centre shows our need for integrity in our day-to-day life.

Ceremony
When we dream of taking part in a ceremony, we are conscious of a new attitude or skill that is needed or an important major life change that is taking place in our lives. We may need new order in our lives, or a deeper sense of awareness, and this is symbolised by a ceremony.

Chain
To dream of chains indicates a type of restriction or dependency. The links in a chain can very often symbolise the communication we need to free ourselves from stifling attitudes. Bondage and slavery, dignity and unity are all symbolised by chains and highlight their ambiguity.

Charity
To dream of giving or receiving charity has a lot to do with our ability to give and receive love and care. Charity comes from the word 'caritas', which means 'caring from the heart'.

Chased
This is a common dream and it often has to do with escaping responsibility or any sense of fear or failure we may have. To be chased by an animal generally indicates we have not come to terms with our own passion.

Chasm
When dreaming of a chasm we are being alerted to situations which hold unknown elements or are in some way risky. We will need to face the situation and eventually make decisions one way or another.

Chess
The game of chess originally signified the 'war' between good and evil. So in dreams it may still express the conflict within. It may also indicate the need for strategy in our lives. Playing chess and losing indicates that we

have undertaken an activity in our waking lives that cannot be successful. We have not got the wherewithal, or perhaps the knowledge, to pit ourselves against greater forces.

Child (who could be one of the dreamer's own children)

Dreaming of a child gives us access to our own inner child. We all have parts of ourselves which are still child-like and inquisitive. When we are able to get in touch with that side of ourselves we give ourselves permission to clarify a capacity for wholeness which we may not previously have recognised.

Chimney

Any opening in a roof represents an awareness of change and growth. It symbolises an escape from the ordinary. On another level, a chimney and the passage of smoke portray the channelling of energy in a more productive way than is presently occurring.

Choking

When we find ourselves choking in a dream we are coming up against our inability to express ourselves appropriately. There is some conflict between our inner and outer selves, perhaps some indecision over whether we should speak out or remain silent. It is also possible that we are being stifled by people or circumstances and are not in control of either.

Christmas Tree

For most people the Christmas Tree is associated with a time of celebration, so to have one appear in a dream signifies the marking of a particular period of time, perhaps a new beginning; a time of giving, and by association the ability to enjoy the 'present'. It may represent the lightening of a situation that has been either oppressive or depressive.

City

Dreaming of a city indicates that we are trying to comprehend our sense of community or neighbourhood. We need to socially or emotionally interact better. A deserted city portrays our feelings of having been neglected by others.

Cliff

To be on the edge of a cliff in a dream indicates the dreamer is facing danger. It shows the need to make a decision as to how to deal with a situation, and possibly be open to taking a risk. We are often facing the unknown. There may be a step we need to take which will psychologically put us either on edge or on the edge in such a way that we must overcome our own fears in order to proceed through our own limitations.

Climbing

To dream of climbing is to dream of getting away from something, possibly of escaping – we may even be avoiding trouble. It also suggests that we are trying to reach new heights in our lives, possibly having to make greater efforts than before to succeed. On another plane, climbing symbolises spiritual ascension, in the sense of climbing to achieve enlightenment.

Cloak

A cloak can suggest warmth and love, but also protection. This protection can be either physical or emotional, or the spiritual protection of faith. Fear of losing the cloak can suggest the fear of losing faith or belief.

Clock

When a clock appears in a dream we are being alerted to the passage of time. We may need to pay more attention to our own sense of timing or duty, or may need to recognise that there is a sense of urgency in what we are doing. If the clock hands arc noticeable they may be indicating those numbers that are important to us. If an alarm clock rings we are being warned of danger.

Clouds

There are various meanings in dreams about clouds. One indicates an uplifting experience; another can indicate that we are feeling overshadowed by someone; and a third may also suggest that we have a hidden depression that can be dealt with only after it has been given form in a dream.

Club – People

When we dream of being in a night club we are highlighting the right of every human being to belong. Psychologically we are not able to be part of a group until we have a certain level of maturity, so to dream of being with a crowd can denote our awareness of ourselves.

Club – Weapon

To dream of using a weapon to club someone denotes an inner violence that has remained unexpressed. It may also depict our violence against ourselves. Conversely, we have great strength at our disposal, for which we need to find an outlet. On another level, a club signifies masculinity, although somewhat crudely expressed.

Coffin

When we dream of a coffin, we are reminding ourselves of our own mortality. We may also be coming to terms with the death of a relationship and feelings of loss. We are also, perhaps, shutting our own feelings away, and therefore causing a part of ourselves to die. On another level redemption, resurrection and salvation are all personified by the coffin.

Cold

To be conscious of cold in a dream is to be aware of feeling neglected, or of being left out of things. We can very often translate our inner feelings or our emotions into a physical feeling in dreams – to feel cold is one such translation.

Colours

Black: This colour holds within it all colour in its potential. It suggests materialisation, pessimism and judgement

Blue: It is the colour of the clear blue sky. This is the most effective healing colour. It suggests relaxation, sleep and tranquility.

Brown: The colour of the earth, death and promise.

Green: This is the colour of equilibrium and compatibility. It is the colour of nature and of plant life.

Grey: There is probably no true grey. It means dedication and service.

Magenta: This is in some ways a colour which links both the physical and the spiritual. It signifies surrender, altruism, perfection and meditative practice.

Orange: This is an essentially cheerful, uplifting colour. The qualities associated are satisfaction and autonomy.

Red: Vitality, strength, dynamism, life, sensuality and power are all connected with this colour. A beautiful clear mid-red is the correct one for these qualities, so if there is any other red in dreams the attributes may not be totally uncontaminated.

Turquoise: The colour is clear greeny-blue. This is taken in some religions to be the colour of the freed soul. It also means rest and simplicity.

Violet: This colour, while found by some to be too strong, means grandeur, esteem and hope. It's purpose is to uplift.

White: The colour containing within it all colours, it suggests innocence, spiritual purity and wisdom.

Yellow: This colour is the one which is closest to daylight. Connected with the emotional self, the attributes are reasoning, sometimes listlessness and judgement.

Compass

Dreaming of a compass means we are attempting to find a direction or activity. We need to be able to understand the differing directions offered to us, and to follow the one that is right for us.

Sometimes having the same significance as the circle, the compass can also represent the source of life, or sometimes justice. On another plane, when we are trying to find direction, and sometimes our own limitations and boundaries, we need a compass.

Contraceptive – *see* Sex

Cooking

If we are cooking in a dream, then we are trying to satisfy a hunger – it may be ours, it may be someone else's. Also, it does not have to be a physical hunger. Cooking can suggest the need to blend certain parts of our life with a view to success; after all, cooking is creative.

Cord

Within any relationship there are certain restrictions and dependencies that become apparent, and these may be depicted in dreams as cords or ties. These emotional bonds can be both limiting and freedom-giving. There is a need to be appreciative of the ties of duty and affection. On another level, there is the symbolism of the Silver Cord – the subtle energy that holds the life force within the body.

Corn

Corn or wheat symbolise fertility or fruitfulness. They may also represent new life or new developments. To be harvesting corn is to be reaping rewards. We may be linking with very primeval needs and requirements. The Great Mother in her nurturing aspect is always shown with corn.

Corner

If we turn a corner in a dream, then we have moved forward into a new experience or phase of our life. If we can note the direction, then turning a right hand corner indicates a logical course of action; to turn a left hand one indicates a more intuitive approach.

Corridor/Hall/Passage

When we dream of being in a corridor we are usually in a state of transition; possibly moving from one state of mind to another, or perhaps between two states of being. We may be in a poor situation, but not be able to make decisions except to accept the inevitable.

Any passage can stand for the passages within the body, the vagina or the anus, the intestines and so on. Equally, on a psychological level, they signify how we allow our personal space to be penetrated. Passages also represent the transitions between the various stages of our lives.

Countryside

Dreaming of countryside puts us in touch with our own natural spontaneous feelings. It can help us to relax or provoke a certain mood. The countryside may also signify a need to clarify our own feelings about our lifestyle – particularly in terms of freedom. The forces of 'nature' in us can be symbolised by scenes of the countryside.

Cradle

To dream of a cradle can represent new life or new beginnings or, for a woman, pregnancy. In a man's dream a cradle can represent the need to return to a womb-like, protected state. An empty cradle can represent a woman's fear of childlessness or her fears of motherhood, depending on the other aspects of the dream. On another level, the physical as opposed to the spiritual body is sometimes represented as a cradle.

Crack

There may be a weakness or a flaw in our lives and this is symbolised by the notion of a crack appearing in a dream. It can also represent the irrational or unexpected. Another meaning is our inability to mentally keep it together.

Cross – *see* Religious Imagery *and* Shapes

Crossing

To dream of crossing a road is recognising the possibility of danger or fear. We are perhaps pitting ourselves against the majority, or something that is bigger than us. To be crossing a field could suggest having a false sense of security – we may need to bring our feelings out into the open. On another plane, crossing a river or chasm often depicts death, not necessarily a physical death but possibly a spiritual change.

Crossroads

Dreaming of crossroads indicates that we are going to have to make choices in our lives, often to do with career or life changes. Turning left at a crossroads can indicate taking the wrong route, though it can indicate the more intuitive path. To turn right can obviously mean taking the correct path, and can also mean making logical decisions.

Crowd

Dreaming of being in a crowd can symbolise the fact that we do not wish to stand out, or that we do not have a sense of direction at present – we may wish to camouflage our feelings from others. We may need to retain our anonymity, to create a facade for ourselves.

Crown

To dream of a crown is to acknowledge one's own success, and to recognise that we have opportunities that will expand our knowledge and awareness. It may indicate that we are about to receive an honour of some sort. The crown can represent victory, and dedication, particularly to duty: also victory over death, suggesting spiritual attainment.

Crutch

When we dream of crutches we are experiencing the need for support, although it may also be that we need to support others. We may find others inadequate and need to readjust our thinking. We may disapprove of other people's shortcomings or weakness. We become aware of our various dependencies: such as alcohol and drugs and even our patterns of behaviour or the people in our lives.

Crucifixion – *see* Religious Imagery

Cube – *see* Shapes

Cul-de-sac

When we find ourselves trapped in a cul-de-sac it symbolises futile action, but perhaps also a state of idleness. Circumstance may be preventing a forward movement, and it may be necessary to retrace one's steps in order to succeed. If we are stuck in old patterns of behaviour, then we may be being threatened by past mistakes.

Cup

The cup has much of the symbolism of the chalice, indicating a receptive state that accepts intuitive information. Often the feminine is offering some opportunity from the unconscious. If we are open to the more feminine side we are able to give and receive help and assistance. The feminine awareness of the draught of life, immortality and plenty is intuitively and sensitively used.

Dagger – *see also* **Knife**

The dagger, as a weapon, is usually understood as a symbol of aggression or masculine power. Having the same significance as a knife, it will depend how it is being used as to the interpretation. Used to attack, the dreamer might become aware that he or she has something to eradicate in life. Used to defend suggests that one is being threatened in some way, but can be more assertive in reply. Any attack highlights the vulnerability of the dreamer.

Dam

Any symbol which suggests a bottling up of great energy can be interpreted as a natural expression of difficulty or frustration. The association with water suggests that we may be bottling up our own emotions and drive, or conversely we could be trying to stop somebody else's emotional outburst from happening. When we build a dam we are putting up defences but if a dam is bursting we may feel we have no control over emotional situations around us.

Dance/Dancing

Spiritually, dance signifies the rhythm of life, and the freedom of spirit which comes about through co-ordinated movement. In many cultures dance movements are symbolic of actions which were necessary for survival, such as the conflict with animals, or represented patterns of creativity. Dance is also used to portray extreme emotion, and it is probably this symbolism which comes about most strongly through dreams.

Danger

A dangerous situation in dreams will usually reflect in a graphic, rather exaggerated form the anxieties and dilemmas of everyday life. Dreams can often highlight a danger or insecurity in symbolic form, such as conflict, fire or flood. Often such a dream contains a warning of inappropriate action which may harm ourselves or others. Dreaming of oneself in a dangerous or precarious position can also indicate a spiritual insecurity.

Date – Day

When a particular date is highlighted in a dream, we are either being reminded of something particularly significant – or possibly traumatic – in our lives or perhaps to consider the symbolism of the numbers contained in the date itself.

Date – Fruit

Fruit, and particularly the date, is often associated with fertility and fertility rites. In Roman times dates, because of their luscious taste and spiritual connections, were often used as an aphrodisiac during pre-nuptial activities. Because dates are an exotic fruit, when we dream of dates we are becoming conscious of the need for the rare or exotic in our lives. Equally, we may need sweetness and nurturing. We need to be cared for and looked after in a way that is different from normal.

Dawn

A new dawn can bring a great sense of hope. To dream of a dawn or a new day represents a new beginning or a new awareness in circumstances around us. We are looking for different, perhaps more spiritual, ways of dealing with old situations.

Day

Time has no real meaning in dreams, so to note that time is measurable suggests that we are actually looking at the length of our lives. It will perhaps be a period of time before something can happen. Dreaming of a specific day of the week may also be a way of alerting us to our state of mind.

Death

Death is a transition from an awareness of the gross physical to the more spiritual side of one's nature. To dream of death, particularly one's own, usually heralds some major change in life, the death perhaps of an old outdated way of being, necessitating a move into the unknown. Dreams of death often occur during those periods in life which were formerly handled by ceremonies and rites of passage, such as puberty to adulthood, maturity to old age. Many women dream of death during the menopause, and this is thought to be because the role of mother is no longer valid, and the woman must re-evaluate her life. Because in the past death held great dread, it also depicted catastrophe, in the sense that nothing would ever be the same again. Depending on one's belief, and whether one believed in life after death it was something that had to be experienced and faced up to rather than understood. Dreaming of death therefore often became a symbol for birth, as a way of coping with it. In these present times, as people's attitudes change, death in a dream indicates a challenge which must be confronted. We need to adjust our approach to life and to accept that there can be a new beginning if we have courage.

Defecate – *see* Excrement *and* Body

Demolition

If we are carrying out the demolition we need to be in control, but if someone else is in charge we may feel powerless in the face of change. We may be conscious of a build-up of emotional energy within ourselves which can only be handled by a breakdown of old attitudes and approaches.

Devil

In previous times, the figure of the Devil was one to be feared and hated. It personified evil, and all of those things which cause conflict between higher ideals and the lesser self. As the wilder, more Pagan side of ourselves, the conventionally recognisable figure with horns and a tail will often appear in dreams. It is almost as though it has been given 'life' by the way that people concentrate on it. Once it is understood as something to be confronted, as something belonging to all of us, the Devil loses its potency.

Digging, Excavation – *see also* **Mine**

Often, when we begin the process of learning about ourselves, we need to uncover those parts we have kept hidden, and this is shown in dreams as excavating a hole or digging up an object.

Dinosaur

When we dream of monsters or prehistoric animals we are touching into very basic images which have the power to frighten and amaze us. Because they are considered to be so large, we need to be aware of whether it is their size or their power which is frightening. Urges as basic as this can threaten our existence, by either their size or power.

Dirty

Evil or negative impulses are often shown in dreams as things or people being dirty. To dream of being dirty may indicate that we are not at ease with our own bodily functions. If someone we know has made us dirty it is an indication not to trust that person.

Disk

A computer disk in a dream could suggest a great deal of information and knowledge is available to us. A compact disc can have a similar significance except that its content, being musical, is more recreational than work-oriented. This could indicate that in waking life we need to be aware of our need for relaxation. Divinity and power are represented spiritually by the disk.

Doctor

It will depend what sort of doctor appears in our dream as to the correct interpretation. A surgeon would suggest the need to cut something out of our lives. A physician would indicate that careful consideration should be given to our general state, whereas a psychiatrist signifies the need to look at our mental state. If the doctor is known to us he may stand as an authority figure.

Door

A door in a dream expresses the idea of a movement between two states of being. It can gain us entry into a new phase of life, such as puberty or middle age. There may be opportunities available to us about which we must make deliberate decisions. If the door in the dream is shut or difficult to open it indicates we are creating obstacles for ourselves, whereas if the door is open we can have the confidence to move forward.

Dove
Always taken to mean the bringer of tranquillity after the storm, the peaceful side of man's nature appears in dreams as the dove.

Dragon
There is a heroic part in each of us which must face danger and conflict in order to manage the lower side of our natures and reach our inner resources. Seen as both frightening and yet manageable, the dragon under certain circumstances will represent in us the 'wild' side of ourselves. We must come to terms with our own passions and chaotic beliefs in order to become custodians of our own future

Draught
Typically a cold draught when working psychically indicates a visitation by Spirit. To feel a draught in a dream is to be aware of an external force which could affect us, or a situation we are in. It also suggests a communication from a hidden part of ourselves.

Draughts/Checkers – *see* Games

Driving
The whole of the symbolism of driving in dreams is particularly obvious. It represents our basic urges, wants, needs and ambitions. If we are driving we are usually in control, though we may be aware of our own inadequacies, particularly if we do not drive in everyday life. If we are uncomfortable when someone else is driving we may not believe in that person, and may not wish to be dependent on them. When someone else takes over, we are becoming passive. If we are overtaking the vehicle in front, we are achieving success, but perhaps as an aggressor. When we are overtaken, we may feel someone else has got the better of us. Once

again the way we are in everyday life is reflected in the dream. Our drives, aggressions, fears and doubts are all reflected in our driving.

Drowning – *see also* **Swimming**

We have allowed ourselves to be put in a situation over which we have no control and where we can be overwhelmed by emotions we cannot handle We have an incompetence in being able to handle an emotionally stressful situation around us at the time of the dream. In more esoteric terms drowning symbolises an immersion in the Sea of Life, and therefore a loss of ego.

Drum – *see also* **Musical Instruments**

We may be seeking a more basic form of expression than the normal, everyday methods we use. We are becoming conscious of the natural rhythm which lies behind all life, and using sound and vibration to seek divine truth.

Drunk – *see* **Intoxication**

Eagle

Because the eagle is a bird of prey, in dreams it signifies dominion and superiority. It can also mean keenness and awareness as well as perception and objectivity. If the dreamer identifies with the eagle his own wish to dominate is becoming apparent though there may be some difficulty in reconciling other parts of the dreamer's nature. If the dreamer feels threatened, somebody else may be threatening the status quo.

Earth

In dreams, earth is often a symbol for the natural support and nurturing which we all need. It can also suggest the mechanisms and networks which we have established, and therefore take for granted. If we are trapped in earth, or buried in some way, it may be that the unconscious drives and needs which have been of value now are tending to overwhelm us.

Earthquake

Old opinions, attitudes and relationships may be breaking up and causing concern. There is massive upheaval occurring in our lives which may be on an emotional level. A dream such as this is almost bound to reveal insecurities, but growth can take place, provided we are prepared to get rid of the debris.

East

May indicate that we are looking at the mysterious and religious side of ourselves. We link with instinctual belief as opposed to logical reasoning; we may also be looking towards a new life or a new beginning.

Easter Egg

The Easter Egg tends to be a symbol of spring, and suggests renewal or undeveloped potential. In dreams we are taken back to childhood feelings of promise and wonder. Dreaming of an Easter Egg may also alert us to the passage of time, since the mind will often produce symbols of times and seasons rather than actual dates.

Eating

Being eaten in a dream suggests being attacked by our own – or possibly other people's – emotions and fears. Being eaten by a wild animal shows the likelihood of us being consumed by our more basic, carnal nature or by our internal drives. Hunger is a basic drive and only once such a drive is satisfied can we move forward to satisfying our more aesthetic needs. To be eating in a dream shows that one is attempting to satisfy one's needs or hunger. To refuse food suggests a rejection of growth and the opportunity to change.

Eclipse – *see also* Moon

On a spiritual level, an eclipse in dreams can represent a loss of faith and fears and doubts about our own ability to succeed. Our light is being dimmed by others more able or talented than we are.

Egg

The egg is the symbol of potential, of opportunities yet to come; we have not made fully conscious our natural abilities and are therefore not yet perfect. To be eating an egg in dreams demonstrates the need to take in certain aspects of newness before we can fully explore a different way of life. We may have to stand back and observe before we can undertake new learning experiences.

Ejaculation

The dreamer's attitude to sex and sexuality often becomes apparent in dreams through the sexual act, and to ejaculate in a dream may be an effort to understand negative feelings, such as fear and doubt. It could also indicate a need for release through sexual satisfaction.

Electricity

Electricity symbolises power, and it will depend on the context of the dream which aspect of our energy is being highlighted. To dream of electrical wires is to be aware of the dreamer's capability, which may have had to remain hidden for a time. Dreaming of switches is to be aware of the ability to control. An electric shock suggests that we are not protecting ourselves from danger, and need to be more aware.

Embryo

The core of being is the embryo, an extremely vulnerable part of ourselves, and therefore the centre of Creation. We may have the beginnings of a project in mind, or a new situation developing which needs careful nurturing. We are working towards conscious knowledge.

Employment

Employment dreams are often to do with how we assess our own worth, among our peers, and what we mean by being gainfully employed. This can be as much to do with status as with reward. Such dreams may also have relevance to the way we perform tasks, with a high degree of focus or not, and also to how we perform in teams.

Empty

In a dream where there is emptiness this may reflect a day-to-day lack of pleasure and enthusiasm, or a sense of isolation. There is an inability to realise expectations, and we have nothing left to give us a sense of security. Empty boxes or rooms might signify having got rid of out-dated material, but having nothing to put in its place.

Enchantress

As the negative aspect of the feminine, the enchantress can appear in dreams as a woman meets her self-destructive side. She is to be understood rather than feared.

The enchantress is such a strong image within both the masculine and feminine psyches that she can appear in dreams in many guises. Morgan le Fay in the story of Arthur epitomises the enchantress. She is the feminine principle in its binding and destroying aspect; the evil witch or the beautiful seductress. She has the power to create illusion, and the ability to delude others.

End

When in life we come to an ending there is also usually a new beginning. Thus when we dream of being at the end of a situation the signs are that it has run out of energy, and it is time to move on. Such a dream can suggest the attainment of a goal, or a point where change is inevitable.

Engine

This represents the sexual impulse or instinctive drives, the life force or one's basic motivation. Something wrong with the engine may indicate the beginning of a health problem.

Engineering

Often in dreams engineering will suggest the control and management of the inherent power we have, both within the spiritual and the physical realms. It suggests our ability to create a structure and use forces which are not normally available to us through techniques and mechanical means. These will allow us either to move forward or will make life easier for us. Dreaming of engineering works is to recognise the need for some adjustment in part of our lives.

Enter, entrance

An entrance in a dream has the same relevance as a door, suggesting new areas of experience, the need to make changes, to create new opportunities. It is often worthwhile to note whether the entrance opens inward or outward, since this may give an indication as to how we handle ourselves in states of transition. An entrance which has two parts to it, such as a porch or an airlock, may be interpreted as the need to balance two aspects of ourselves before proceeding.

Escape

Escape suggests our need for spiritual freedom, of attempting to move beyond – or to avoid – difficult feelings. Many anxiety dreams have an element in them of the need to escape, either the situation itself, or something that is threatening us.

We may also be trying to escape from something we know we must tackle, such as a responsibility or duty.

Evening

Evening signifies old age, and wisdom. It also suggests twilight, and the boundaries of our conscious mind. Evening or evening light means that we should take time for ourselves – perhaps relaxation and quiet peace.

Evil

Sensing evil in a dream usually suggests that there is something which is misplaced or corrupt. Evil usually brings with it a sense of dread, foreboding or disgust, particularly if it is accompanied by inappropriate action from other people. To experience evil in a dream is usually to be conscious of our own urges, which we have judged to be wrong.

Exams, being examined – *see also* Tests

Dreaming of taking or being barred from examinations is a fairly typical anxiety dream which has a great deal to do with the standards we set ourselves, and our need for achievement. We have a need to be accepted for what we can do, so some of the occasions which worry us as children are used by the dreaming self to symbolise other such occasions. Being examined by a doctor or an alien may be in the first place alerting us to concerns over health, though this need not necessarily be physical, and in the second our need to come to terms with our sense of our own body.

Excrement – *see also* Body

The power of the person is said to be contained in his excrement, since we often need to let go various aspects and experiences of our loves, in order to make room for the new. Dreaming of experiencing pleasure in our own excrement returns us to an innocent type of self-expression.

Explosion

A dream is a safe space in which to accomplish the cleansing which occurs through the release of anger and fear, and an explosion can symbolise such a process. It enables us to make room for more positive expression of what we are feeling and thinking

Eye – *see* Body

Face

Faces appearing in dreams by themselves often seem to be random snatches of what many might call the psychic or astral content of our dreams. It often strikes us that the faces are particularly beautiful or by contrast hideously ugly, and since there is an element of disembodiment about them we are most likely being alerted to particular types of personality. We may be seeking knowledge or information not otherwise available to us. To concentrate on somebody else's face in a dream is an attempt to understand the outward personality. When the face is hidden from us, which can happen frequently as we choose to begin to develop psychic powers, we can make the assumption that certain information is being hidden from us until we are able to deal with it. We also at that stage probably need to look at how we are presenting ourselves within the everyday world.

Fairground

The fairground has a dreamlike quality all of its own. It is a sort of enclosed world of fantasy, and may alert us to the way in which we handle the childlike aspects of ourselves. Roundabouts might, for instance, suggest the daily round of existence, while swing boats might signify the ups and downs of fortune. The Ferris wheel is often a representation of the Wheel of Life. It is possible that we need to lose some of our inhibitions.

Fairy

Fairies are known to be capricious, and in dreams may represent the spontaneous elemental side of our being. It will obviously depend upon which type of fairy appears in our dreams, since each type will have a different significance. They may suggest mischief, or the more malign side of the coin, as in goblins and elves.

Falcon

The falcon as a bird of prey shares the attributes of the eagle. It embodies freedom and hope for those who are being restricted. It can represent victory over lust, arising from the control imposed on it by its owner.

Fall/Falling

The sensation of falling in dreams can arise during the hypnogogic or hypnopompic states. It may be interpreted as the need to be grounded, to take care within a known situation. Equally we may be harmed by being too pedestrian. Falling has also come to be interpreted as sexual surrender and as moral failure, not being as one should. We may not feel that we are properly in control of our lives.

Fame

The ego craves recognition, and dreaming of being famous or of achieving fame within a chosen field signifies that we ourselves need to recognise and give ourselves credit for our own abilities. If we are trying to make decisions as to how to move forward within our lives, we have to recognise our potential to stand out in a crowd. Being treated as a famous film star suggests our ability to be acknowledged by others, often in a slightly more glamorous way than normally.

Family

Images of the family, being the first people we relate to, have a great deal of significance in dreams.

Dreams about individual members of the family, and their status within it, can involve the symbolism of various archetypes. With that in mind the **father** represents the masculine principle and that of authority, while the mother signifies the nurturing, protective principle.

A **brother** can represent the dual feelings of parity and rivalry. In a man's dream an older brother indicates experience coupled with authority, while a younger, less experienced brother suggests vulnerability and possibly a lack of maturity. In a woman's dream a younger brother represents, again, rivalry, but also vulnerability – whether her own or her brother's. An older brother can denote her confident, outgoing self.

When the relationship with a **daughter** is emphasised in dreams, it often represents the outcome of the relationship between husband and wife. In a woman's dream, the relationship with the daughter suggests a jointly supportive one – although rivalry and jealousy can arise that, of course, needs to be dealt with. In a man's dream his daughter may bring into prominence his fears about his own ability to handle his vulnerability.

When members of the extended family –**cousins, aunts, uncles**, etc. – appear in dreams it typifies the various parts of ourselves that are recognisable.

If the relationship with **father** is a good one in waking life, the image of father in dreams will usually be a positive one. Father also represents authority and all the conventional forms of law and order. In a man's life the father generally becomes a role model, though it is often only when the individual discovers that he is not being true to his own nature that dreams can point the way to a more fruitful life. In a woman's life father is the standard on whom she bases all later relationships. When she appreciates that she no longer needs to use this standard, she is then able to work out in dreams a more suitable way to have a mature relationship. If the relationship with father has been a difficult one, there may be some opposition to resolving the various conflicts that will have arisen – often this can be accomplished in dreams.

Grandparents appearing in dreams denote not only our attitude to them, but also to the traditions and beliefs handed down by them, of which there are usually many. It could be said that grandparents do not know whether they have done a good job of raising their children until their sons and daughters have children of their own.

Within the **husband/wife** relationship lie the crucial feelings a wife has about her own sexuality and intimacy of body, mind and spirit. Her view of herself will have been formed by her connection with her father, and any ensuing relationship will be tinted by that bond. If her doubts about validity are not expressed correctly, they will appear in dreams in the guise of the loss, or death, of her husband. They can, on occasion, also be projected onto other women's husbands.

The **wife/husband** relationship is based on how good the man perceives himself to be as a husband or the woman as wife. If he has formed a relatively good, if not entirely successful, relationship with his mother, he will try to prove himself a good husband through his dreams. He will also experience the potential loss and death of his partner in the same way as he experienced the loss in emotional terms of his mother.

Primary in a child's development is its relationship with **mother.** In the main it is the first relationship that the child develops, and should be perceived by the child as a loving, caring one. If this does not happen, anxiety and mistrust may arise, which can result in men perpetually having relationships with older women, or, in some cases, completely denying the right to any relationship. In a woman's life her ability to relate to others depends on her relationship with her mother. She may feel she has to look after the needy male, or form relationships with both men and women that may not be totally fulfiling. In the use of dreams as therapy there are many ways of working through relationships with the mother figure if one dares; much material and spiritual success can be attained.

The **sister** in dreams represents the feeling, sensitive side of ourselves. Through being able to understand our sister's personality we have the ability to make connections with that part of ourselves. If she is older in a man's dream the sister allows the ability to show the capacity for persecution but also for caring. If she is younger, then she can highlight the more vulnerable side of his personality. Women dreaming of a younger sister suggest some kind of sibling rivalry. If older, the sister stands for aptitude and capability.

The **son** appearing in dreams suggests the dreamer's need for self-expression. He can also signify parental responsibility. In a mother's dream he may characterise her ambitions. In a father's dream he can highlight unfulfilled hopes, dreams and desires, depending on how the dream develops.

Fan

A fan often suggests sensuality and sexuality. There was at one time a recognisable language associated with the fan, so such an article has come to represent the capricious feminine personality.

Particularly in a woman's dream, the fan can be used as a symbol for openness to new experience and creativity. Waving a fan is reputed to clear away evil forces.

Far/Near

In dreams, space and time can become interchangeable. Dreaming of something which is far away, may indicate that it is far away in time. This may be future or past, depending on the dream. A long way in front would be future, a long way behind would be past.

Near or close would mean recently, or, in the here and now.

Fare

A dream in which one is having to pay a fare occurs when one feels that what one has done has not been paid for, and that there is a need to come to terms with the demands that may be being made on us. To be paying a fare in a dream is acknowledging the price that is paid in order to succeed. A taxi fare would be a more private process than a bus fare.

Fat

To dream of being fat alerts the dreamer to the defences used against inadequacy. Equally we may also be conscious of the sensuality and fun side of ourselves we have not used before. Depending on how we think of our bodies in the waking state, we can often use the dream image of ourselves to change the way we feel. Fat also represents a choice part of Spiritual knowledge.

Fax machine, fax

Messages from a hidden source or part of ourselves are often brought to us in dreams in a totally logical way. Thus, while the message itself may be unintelligible, how it is initially received is not. We may be aware that someone is trying to communicate with us but, because we are distanced from them, the transmission has to be mechanical. In a dream, a fax machine can have spiritual undertones in that it can be a way of transmitting messages from 'beyond'.

Feather

Feathers in a dream could denote softness and lightness, perhaps a more gentle approach to a situation. We may need to look at the truth within the particular situation and to recognise that we need to be calmer in what we are doing. Feathers often represent flight to other parts of the

Self, and because of their connection with the wind and the air, can represent the more spiritual side of ourselves. To see feathers in a dream perhaps means that we have to complete an action before allowing ourselves to rest.

Fence
Dreaming of fences signifies that we are aware of boundaries – maybe class or social – it could also be a boundary within a relationship. It may be that we find it hard to express ourselves, in which case we need to put in a bit more effort.

Ferry
To dream of being on a ferry indicates that we are making some movement towards change. Because the ferry carries large numbers of people it may also represent a group to which we belong that needs to make changes. The ferry is associated with death; there is the story of being ferried across the River Styx to death. This would indicate a major change is on its way.

Field
When we dream that we are in a field we are looking more at our field of activity, that is, what we are doing in everyday life. It may also be a play on words in that it is to do with the feeling state and is to do with the freedom from social pressure. It may also be an indication that we need to get back to nature, to basics as it were.

Fig
The fig, because of its shape, is connected to sexuality, fertility, masculinity and prosperity. If we are eating figs in a dream, then it may be that a celebration is in order. The fig is also associated with the Tree of Knowledge and the deeper awareness that comes with that. On another level, it can represent a psychic ability and a direct connection with the beginning of physical life.

Fight
If we dream that we are in a fight, it usually indicates that we are

confronting our need for independence. We may also need to express our anger and frustration and the subconscious desire to hurt a part of ourselves.

File

Dreaming of an abrasive file – such as a metal file – would suggest that we are capable of being too abrasive with people.

In modern times to dream of files or filing and thus putting order into our lives is to make sense of what we are doing and how we are doing it. A chaotic situation can now be dealt with in an orderly manner.

Film

To dream of being at a film indicates we are viewing an aspect of our own past or character that needs to be acknowledged in a different way. We are attempting to view ourselves objectively or perhaps we may be escaping from reality. Film as recording images is an important part of modern man's make-up and to be put in a position of viewing film within a dream is to be creating a different reality from the one we presently have. If we are making a film, (if it is not our normal occupation) we may need to question the reality we are creating.

Fire

Fire in a dream can suggest passion and desire in its more positive sense, and frustration, anger, resentment and destruction in its more negative. It will depend on whether the fire is controlled or otherwise as to the exact interpretation. To be more conscious of the flame of the fire would be to be aware of the energy and strength that is created. Being aware of the heat of a fire is to be aware of someone else's strong feelings. Psychologically, fire often appears in dreams as a symbol of cleansing and purification. We can use the life-giving and generative power to change our lives.

Sometimes fire indicates the need to use our sexual power to good effect. To dream of being burnt alive may express our fears of a new relationship or phase of life. We may also be conscious of the fact that we could suffer for our beliefs. Baptism by fire signifies a new awareness of spiritual power and transformation.

Fireworks

Fireworks are generally accepted as belonging to a happy occasion or celebration, though they may also be frightening. So when we dream of fireworks we are hoping to be able to celebrate good fortune, although it may be tempered by another emotion. Fireworks can have the same significance as an explosion. A release of energy or emotion can have quite a spectacular effect on us, or on people around us. In another meaning there could be an excess of spiritual emotion that needs to be channelled properly.

Fish

To dream of fish links in with our emotions – more specifically our ability to be wise without being methodical. We should all have awareness and knowledge, and dreaming of fish indicates that the common experience, as it were, is now more available to us than ever. Two fish swimming in opposite directions represents Pisces.

Flag – *see also* Banner

A flag in a dream will have the same meaning as a banner, that is, a standard or a place round which people with common aims and beliefs can gather. It may represent old fashioned principles and beliefs.

Fleas

Fleas are an irritation, and in dreams signify just that. There may be people or situations in our lives that are causing us difficulty and we need to go through a process of decontamination in order to be free.

We may be aware that we are not being treated properly and that people who should be our friends are not being fair. Fleas are symbolic of the type of evil that is likely to hurt, rather than destroy – such as gossip. The dreamer should be aware that he can deal with it.

Fleece

We may be word associating as in the sense of being 'fleeced' or cheated. The fleece of a sheep also represents security, warmth and comfort, and will often signify those creature comforts we are able to give ourselves or others.

Flies

Flies are always associated with something nasty, which does not allow for the fact that they also devour rotten material. So to dream of flies is to be aware that we have certain negative aspects of our lives that need dealing with.

Flight/Flying

Conventionally, to dream of flying is to do with sex and sexuality, but it would probably be more accurate to look at it in terms of lack of inhibition and freedom. We are releasing ourselves from limitations that we may impose on ourselves. To be flying upwards is to be moving towards a more spiritual appreciation of our lives, while to be flying downwards is to be making an attempt to understand the sub-conscious and all that entails.

Floating

Floating in a dream was considered by Freud to be connected with sexuality, but it is probable that it is much more to do with the inherent need for freedom. Generally we are opening to power beyond our conscious self, when we are carried along apparently beyond our own volition. We are in a state of extreme relaxation and are simply allowing events to carry us along. Because we are not taking charge of our own direction, we are being indecisive and perhaps need to think more carefully about our actions and involvements with other people.

Flood

Although flood dreams are sometimes frightening they mostly indicate a release of positive energy. Often it is an overflow of repressed feelings, which, if we are in the middle of a flood, are also feelings that we have been overwhelmed by. Flood dreams do sometimes suggest depression.

Flowers

Flowers in a dream usually give us the opportunity to link to feelings of pleasure and beauty. We are aware that something new, perhaps a feeling or ability, is beginning to come into being and that there is a freshness about what we are doing. To be given a bouquet means that we are being rewarded for an action – the colour of the flowers may be important (See **Colours**). Formerly each individual flower had a meaning in dreams: **Anemone** Your present partner is untrustworthy. **Arum Lily** An unhappy marriage or the death of a relationship. **Bluebell** Your partner will become argumentative. **Buttercup** Your business will increase. **Carnation** A passionate love affair. **Clover** Someone who is in need of finance will try to get in touch. **Crocus** A dark man around you is not to be trusted. **Daffodil** You have been unfair to a friend; look for reconciliation. **Forget-me-not** Your chosen partner cannot give you what you need. **Forsythia** You are glad to be alive. **Geranium** A recent quarrel is not as serious as you thought. **Honeysuckle** You will be upset by domestic quarrels. **Iris** Hopefully, you will receive good news. **Lime/Linden** This suggests feminine grace. **Marigold** There may be business difficulties. **Mistletoe** Be constant to your lover. **Myrtle** This gives joy, peace, tranquillity, happiness and constancy. **Narcissus** Take care not to mistake shadow for substance. **Peony** Excessive self restraint may cause you distress. **Poppy** A message will bring great disappointment. **Primrose** You will find happiness in a new friendship. **Rose** Indicates love and perhaps a wedding, within a year. **Snowdrop** Confide in someone and do not hide your problems. **Violet** You will marry someone younger than yourself.

Flute – *see also* **Music/Musical Instruments**

Many musical instruments – particularly wind instruments – indicate extremes of emotion, enticement and flattery. Because of the shape the flute is often taken as a symbol of masculine virility, but could also be taken to stand for anguish.

As a way of expressing the sound of the spirit, and therefore harmony, the flute can be used as a symbol of happiness and joy. It may also indicate celestial music and all that's associated with it.

Fog

To dream of being in a fog marks our confusion and inability to confront, or even to see, the real issues at stake. To be walking in a fog is often a warning that matters we consider important can be clouded by other people's judgement and it may be wiser to sit still and do nothing.

Food – *see also* **Eating and Nourishment**
Our need and enjoyment of food fulfils certain inherent needs. The meanings of some foods are as follows: **Bread** We are looking at our experiences and our basic needs. **Cake** This signifies sensual enjoyment. **Fruits** We are representing in dream form the fruits of our experience or effort, and the potential for prosperity. The colour could also be significant. **Ham/Cured Meat** Our need for preservation is represented by cured meats. **Meals** Depending on whether we are eating alone or in a group meals can indicate acceptance and sociability. **Meat** Physical or worldly satisfaction or needs are shown in dreams as meat. Raw meat can supposedly signify impending misfortune. **Milk** As a basic food, milk will always signify baby needs and giving to oneself. **Onion** The different layers of oneself are often shown as an onion *(see also individual entry)*. **Sweets** These tend to represent sensual pleasure. **Vegetables** These represent our basic needs and material satisfaction. They also suggest the goodness we can take from the Earth and situations around us. The colour may also be important *(see* **Colours***)*.

Footprints
To see footprints in a dream indicates that we are needing to follow someone. If those footprints are stretching in front of us there is help available in the future, but if they are behind us, then perhaps we need to look at the way we have done things in the past. Footprints usually indicate help in one way or another and certainly consideration. If we see footprints going in opposite directions we need to consider what has happened in the past and what is going to happen in the future.

Forest
Dreaming of forests or a group of trees usually means entering the realms of the feminine. A forest is often a place of testing and initiation. It is always something to do with coming to terms with our emotional self, of understanding the secrets of our own nature.

Fork
A fork, particularly a three pronged one, is often considered to be the symbol of the Devil and therefore can symbolise evil and trickery. In

dreams a fork denotes duality and indecision. Psychologically, the fork can signify the same as a barb or a goad – something that is driving us, often to our own detriment. We may have come to a fork on our spiritual path and development and need guidance as to which direction to take.

Forge

When the forge and the blacksmith were a part of normal, everyday life this particular dream would indicate some aspect of hard work or desire to reach a goal. Now it is more likely to mean a ritual action. The forge represents the masculine and active force. It also represents the power of transmuting that which is base and unformed into something sacred. To dream of a forge indicates that we are changing internally and allowing our finer abilities to be shown.

Forward/Backward

A forward and/or backward movement indicates the possibility of taking a retrograde, backward-looking stance. There is a need or a tendency to retire into the past, rather than tackling fears and moving ahead.

Fountain

To dream of a fountain means that we are aware of the process of life and 'flow' of our own consciousness. Because of its connection with water it also represents the surge of our emotions, and often our ability to express this. The fountain can also represent an element of play in our lives, the need to be free-flowing and untroubled.

Fraud

When fraud appears in a dream, particularly if the dreamer is being defrauded, there is the potential to be too trusting. If the dreamer is the one committing fraud, he or she runs the risk of losing a good friend.

Friend

A friend appearing in our dreams can signify one of two things. Firstly we need to look at our relationship with that particular person, and secondly we need to decide what that friend represents for us (for instance: security, support, and love). Often friends highlight a particular part of our own personality that we need to look at, and perhaps understand or come to terms with, in a different way.

Front/Back
Acceptance and rejection can be shown in a dream as seeing the front and back of something.

Funeral
A funeral indicates the need to come to terms with our feelings about death or a time of mourning for something that has happened in the past and this time of mourning can allow us to move forward. Dreaming of one's parents' funeral indicates a move towards independence.

Furniture
The furniture which appears in our dreams, particularly if it is drawn to our attention, often shows how we feel about our family and home life, and what attitudes or habits we have developed. It can also give an indication as to how we feel about ourselves. For instance, dark heavy material would suggest the possibility of depression, whereas brightly painted objects could testify to an upbeat mentality.

Sometimes the furniture which appears in a dream can highlight our need for security or stability, particularly if it is recognisable from the past.

Different articles can represent different attitudes:

Bed, Mattress This can show exactly what is happening in the subtle areas of our close relationships. We can get an insight into how we really feel about intimacy and sexual pleasure. For some people the bed is a place of sanctuary and rest, where they can be totally alone. **Carpet** Often when carpets appear in a dream we are looking at our emotional links with finance. The colour of the carpet should be noted. **Chair** A chair can indicate that we need a period of rest and recuperation. We may need to deliberately take time out, to be open to other opportunities. **Cupboard, Wardrobe** Cupboards and wardrobes may depict those things we wish to keep hidden, but may also depict how we deal with the different roles we must play in life. **Table** For a table to appear in a dream is often to do with communal activity, and with one's social affiliations (*see also individual entry and* **Altar** *under* **Religious Imagery**).

Gale − *see also* **Wind**

Being in a gale in dreams indicates that we are being buffeted by circumstances that we feel are beyond our control. We have got ourselves into circumstances over which we have no control. We must make decisions as to whether we are going to confront the forces of nature, or perhaps our own inner spirituality, and harness the energy that we have, in order to fulfil a task.

Games

Playing any game in our dream indicates that we are taking note of how we play the game of life. If we are playing well we may take it that we are coping well with circumstances in our lives. If we are playing badly we may need to reassess our abilities and to identify which skills we need to improve in order to do things better. Games and gambling can also represent not taking life seriously. They can show how we work within the competitive field and give us some kind of insight into our own sense of winning or losing.

Specific games such as football, baseball, rugby and cricket, which are team games, represent for many the strong ability to identify with a 'tribe' or a group of people. Because they are mock fights they can be used as expressions of aggressiveness against other people, in the way that wars and localised tribal fights were used previously. They indicate the way in which we gain identity and how we connect with people. In dreams, games which require the power of thought and strategy − such as chess or draughts − often give some idea of how we should be taking a situation forward (*see* **Chess**). Decisions may need to be made where we have to gauge the result of our action, and take into account our opponent's reaction. To dream of gambling indicates that we may need to look at something in our lives that is figuratively a gamble; we may need to take risks, but in such a way that we have calculated the risks as best we can.

Garage

A garage is the workshop from which we move out into the world, having done what we need to do in order to repair and conserve the symbols of our success. In dreams a garage is representative of the way we look after and maintain our drive and motivation, and how we look after the resources that we have.

If we are having to pay a visit to a professional garage, it can suggest an expertise that we do not have, or that a source of energy needs to be properly maintained.

Garbage

Garbage or rubbish in our dream suggests that there are certain parts of our lives that can now be thrown away or discarded. We have perhaps still retained 'left over' feelings and concepts that may have nurtured us in the past but no longer do so. It will often depend on the type of garbage that is being thrown away as to the symbolism. The remains of food preparation would make us look at nurturing, while throwing out old furniture might suggest discarding something that no longer brings comfort.

Garden

In dreams a garden can represent a form of paradise, as in the Garden of Eden, and is often a symbol of the feminine and qualities of wildness.

Dreaming of a garden can be illuminating, because it can indicate areas of potential growth in our own lives, or it can be that which we are trying to cultivate in ourselves.

Dreaming of a closed garden suggests virginity. It often signifies the inner life of the dreamer and that which we totally appreciate about our own being.

Garland

Psychologically a garland can represent honour and recognition, some sort of accolade for work done or a task completed. Such a thing in dreams would suggest approval by one's peers, rather than self-congratulation. Garlands as decoration of a space or building are a rather old fashioned representation of a time of celebration and merriment. The type of garland may also be important.

Garlic

Garlic in olden times had a great deal of importance, particularly in the use of magic. It was often seen as a symbol of masculine fertility and because of its smell it was seen as protection against evil forces. Dreaming of garlic may therefore connect back to either of these meanings, unless of course it is being used in cooking when the meaning may be altered by the symbolism of the other ingredients.

Gas

Gas can have the same significance as air and wind in dreams but usually is taken to be slightly more dangerous. It may suggest intellectual power, which when controlled is useful but dangerous when misused. As something supplied to us from an external source it is a precious useable commodity, which requires discretion and thought in its application. To dream of not being able to turn the gas on, for instance, would suggest that there is a lack of energy in a particular project.

Gate

A gate in dreams signifies passing through some kind of barrier or obstacle in order to continue on our way. It marks a transition or change from one stage of life to another. It also signifies a change in awareness. Often the awareness of change is highlighted by the type of gate. For instance, a utilitarian gate such as a factory one would tend to indicate a work change, whereas a garden gate might represent pleasure. The gate between the physical and spiritual realms has a long established existence.

Genitals – *see also* Body

The child becomes aware of his or her own genitals, particularly as a source of pleasure, at a very early age, so to dream of one's own genitals could suggest a need for childlike comfort, or some problem with one's own sexuality. To dream of being mutilated around the genitals could refer to either past or present abuse, either sexual or emotional, or a blow to one's self-esteem. Dreaming of someone else's genitals either indicates our involvement with that person's sexuality, or, if of the opposite sex, our need to understand the hidden side of ourselves.

Giant

Giants and ogres in dreams often represent an emotion that is big and uncontrollable. It is often unconfined primordial power, and takes us back to the helplessness we may have experienced as a child in an adult world. We may also become conscious of ourselves as being larger than life as we begin to develop spiritually, and need to become aware of the shifts in perspective that are necessary. Dreaming of giants helps us to handle such change without too much trauma.

Gift – *see also* **Present**

In a spiritual sense, dreaming of a gift may be highlighting our creative talents, of which we may not have been aware. To receive a gift within a dream is to recognise our talents and abilities. Each of us has a store of unconscious knowledge which from time to time becomes available, often through dreams. Depending on the circumstances, we are acknowledging what we receive from others.

Gig

Today, the gig, concert, or rave has taken the place of the dance or tea party. In dreams, therefore, it can represent an opportunity for freedom and movement, a social occasion or a gathering of people who are on the same wavelength as ourselves. This then signifies our need for us to 'let go', if only for a short time.

Girdle

A girdle represents wisdom, strength and power, and also the inevitability of the cycle of life and death. In a woman's dream the girdle may depict her sense of her own femininity, for instance whether she feels bound or constricted by it. In a man's dream it is more likely to show his understanding of his power over his own life.

Girl

When a girl of any age appears in our dreams we are attempting to make contact with the more sensitive, innocent, intuitive side of ourselves. If the girl is known to us we are aware of those qualities, but need to explore them more fully. If unknown, we can accept a fresh approach is useful.

Girlfriend

When a girlfriend or ex-girlfriend appears in a man's dream there are usually matters to do with the relationship between the masculine and feminine, whether in the dreamer himself or in his environment. There may also be fears to do with sexuality. If a girlfriend appears in a woman's dream, there can either be a concern about her in the dreamer's mind, or she (the dreamer) needs to search for – and find – qualities belonging to the friend within herself.

Glass

Glass is a barrier but it is transparent and therefore allows us to see that which we cannot reach. If we dream of breaking glass we are probably ready to break free from emotional ties and enter a new phase in our lives. Any barriers that we or others put up can be dealt with successfully. Glass also signifies the barrier between life and the hereafter.

Glasses, Spectacles

Glasses or spectacles indicate an association with our ability to see or to understand. Psychologically, when we are able to wear glasses we are more able to look at that which is external to ourselves rather than turning inwards and becoming introspective. In the spiritual sense, a dream of glasses or spectacles may be urging us to take a different viewpoint. Equally, if someone is unexpectedly wearing glasses, it is to do either with our lack of understanding or perhaps their inability to see where we are coming from.

Globe

A globe symbolises our need for wholeness or the approach to wholeness To dream of looking at a globe, particularly in the sense of a world globe, indicates our acknowledgement of the need for a wider viewpoint. We can cultivate a more globally aware perspective. We have certain powers within us that will enable us to create a sustainable future for all, and for this we need to be able to understand and take a world view.

Goat

The goat is the symbol for Capricorn in the Zodiac. In its more negative aspect it signifies the darker side of human nature, immorality and over sexuality. More positively, dreaming of a goat is to recognise creative energy and masculine vigour. The goat may also be taken to represent the Devil.

Goal

To dream of scoring a goal may indicate that we have set ourselves external targets. In achieving those targets we may also recognise that the goals that we have set ourselves in life are either short or long term and we may need to adjust them in some way. If we miss a goal, then we may need to reassess our abilities to make the grade – but we can still aspire to great things.

Goblet

In dreams the goblet represents the feminine, receptive principle and our ability to achieve enjoyment in a number of different ways. We may be able to make a celebration out of something that is quite ordinary. To be drinking from a goblet indicates we are allowing ourselves the freedom to enjoy life to the full. To dream of a set of goblets indicates that there are several different ways in which we can make our lives enjoyable and fun.

Gold

Gold signifies the best, most valuable aspects of ourselves. Finding gold indicates that we can discover those characteristics in ourselves or others. Burying gold shows that we are trying to hide something. Gold in dreams can also represent the sacred, dedicated side of ourselves. We can recognise incorruptibility and wisdom, love and patience. In this context it seldom stands for material wealth, being more the spiritual assets that one has.

Gong

If we are a gong sounding, then we need to recognise that a limitation has been reached, or that we are summoned to success. If we are striking the gong. then this represents a need for strength. Overall a gong symbolises that something requires recognition.

Grail

The Holy Grail is such a key image that in dreams it can appear as something miraculous, something that fulfils our wish and allows us to move forward into our full potential. Often it signifies the achievement of spiritual success, but can also represent the cup of happiness. The grail appearing in a dream indicates that we can expect some form of satisfaction and change to occur within our lives. We are searching for something that we may feel is unattainable, but by putting ourselves through various tests may eventually be attainable.

Grain

Dreaming of grain can indicate some kind of a harvest. We have created opportunities for ourselves in the past that now can come to fruition. Provided we look after the outcome of these opportunities, we can take that success forward and create even more abundance. To dream of grain growing in a field can indicate that we are on the point of success, that we have tended our lives sufficiently to be able to achieve growth.

Grasshopper

The grasshopper is a symbol of freedom and capriciousness, and in dreams it can often indicate a bid for freedom. The expression 'a grasshopper mind' shows an inability to settle to anything, and will be seen in dreams as a grasshopper. On another level, in Chinese history the grasshopper is often associated with enlightenment.

Grave – *see also* Death

Dreaming of a grave indicates that we must have regard for our feelings about, or our concept of, death. We may also be attempting to deal with our feelings about someone who has died – part of our personality may have been killed off, or is dead and buried to the outside world.

Grease

In a dream, grease is the word that indicates that we have not taken as much care over a situation as we should have. It suggests that we should use better judgement lest we put ourselves at unnecessary risk. Grease can also signify making things easier for ourselves.

Guillotine

A guillotine in a dream indicates something irrational in our personality. We may be afraid of losing self-control. We could be aware of an injury to our person or to our dignity. There is the potential for us to lose contact with someone we love, or with the part of ourselves that is capable of love. By way of its physical action, a guillotine represents a severance of some kind.

Guitar

Guitar music in a dream can indicate the possibility of a new romance, but can also indicate the need for caution. If the dreamer is playing the guitar he or she is making an attempt to be more creative. Any musical instrument characterises our need for rest, relaxation and harmony.

Gun

In dreams the gun has masculine and sexual connotations. If a woman is firing a gun she is aware of the aggressive side of her personality. If she is being shot at she perhaps feels threatened by overt sexuality. It will depend on the circumstances in the dream as to how we interpret the use of a gun. We may be using it as a protection of those things we feel are important to us. The symbolism here reverts to a more base attribute – that of straightforward masculinity.

Guru

A guru appearing in a dream is a representation of the wisdom of the unconscious. As that wisdom becomes available we often bring it through to conscious knowledge. Psychologically, we all need a symbol for a father figure and this is one such symbol. In searching for knowledge of a specific sort, we need an external figure with whom to relate. In Eastern religions, this is the guru – who performs the same function as the priest in Western religion. For many of us, God is too remote for us to be able to have a personal relationship with him. A guru therefore becomes the personification of all wisdom made available to us through his perception. He will assist us to access our own innate wisdom.

Hail

Because it is frozen water, hail signifies the freezing of our emotions. It would appear that the damage created by these frozen emotions comes from outside influences rather than internal feelings. Hail has a particular part to play in the cycle of nature. We need to appreciate that there are times when numbing our emotions may be appropriate – though not indefinitely.

Hair – *see also* Body

Ham – *see also* Food

Hammer

Dreaming of hammers indicates a more aggressive, masculine side of our nature. There may be the feeling that part of our personality needs to be crushed, supressed or struck in some way for us to be able to operate properly. The double-sided hammer also has symbolism. The two sides are justice and vengeance. The dreamer needs to be aware which one is relevant to them.

Hand – *see* Body

Hanging

Hanging is a violent, sometimes misjudged, act against a person; if we witness a hanging in our dream, then we are open to violence, and perhaps need to reconsider our actions. If we ourselves are being hanged, we are being warned of some problem – possibly the prospect of taking the blame for someone else's actions. Alternatively, there may be a hang-up in our lives. If something is hanging over us, then we are being threatened or suppressed by some circumstance around us.

Hare

Because of its affiliation with the moon, the hare can signify the Priestess/Witch aspect of femininity or the Priest/Sorcerer of the masculine – the intuitive faculty, spiritual insight and instinctive 'leaps'. Madness, however, comes from not using one's powers effectively, leading to illusion. In its positive imagery, it is the radiant hare (often holding its baby in a cave), and thus the Mother of God.

Harem

For a man to dream that he is in a harem suggests that he is struggling to come to terms with the feminine nature. For a woman, it shows that she is understanding her own flamboyant, sensual side. On a different level, she is recognising her need to belong to a group of women – a sisterhood.

Any group of women appearing in dreams will signify femininity in one form or another, and a more detailed interpretation will depend on whether the dreamer relates to a particular person in the scenario.

Harp

Dreaming of a harp indicates that we need to find the correct vibration within our life to create a harmony. If we are 'harping on' then we feel we need to be listened to or acknowledges. The harp sometimes signifies the ladder to the next world.

Harvest

We are going to reap the rewards of all the hard work we've put in – if the symbolism for harvest has its way. To dream of a harvest can actually have two meanings. In can mean looking back into the past and reaping the rewards, or it can mean looking towards the future in order to use what has happened previously.

Head – *see* Body

Hearse

Obviously linked to death, the hearse lso reveals concern about a time limitation. It may also be that time is running out, not necessarily for us, but for a project or relationship. It may be best to let matters lie rather than try any kind of resurrection.

Heart – *see* **Body**

Hearth
To dream of a hearth or fireplace is to recognise the need for security. This may be of two different types. One is knowing that the home is secure and a safe environment. The other is recognising the security of the inner self. We may be, or need to be, linking with our own passionate wilder nature.

Heaven – *see* **Religious Imagery**

Heel – *see* **Body**

Hell – *see* **Religious Imagery**

Hen
The hen denotes discretion, mothering and procreation. When a hen crows in a dream it is taken to represent feminine domination.

Hermit
There is a type of loneliness within many people that prevents them from making relationships on a one-to-one basis. This may manifest in dreams as the figure of the hermit. In dreams if we meet the hermit on a journey, we are discovering the dimension in ourselves that has a spiritual awareness.

Hero/Heroine
In a man's dream the figure of the hero can represent all that is good in him, the Higher Self. In a woman's dream he will suggest the Animus. When the hero is on a quest, the dreamer is struggling to find a part of him or herself which is at this time unconscious (*see also* **Quest**). It is important that the darker forces in oneself are conquered – but not annihilated, since they cannot be totally eradicated without harming the

'Wise Old Man'. In other words, our eventual integration still needs the challenge of the negative. In dreams the hero's failure may be brought about inadvertently. We all have a weak point through which we can be attacked, and we may be being warned of an element of self-neglect. To have such a dream indicates that we are not paying attention to the details in our lives or to that part of ourselves we tend not to have developed. The death of the hero can often suggest the need to develop the more intuitive side of ourselves, to be born again to something new. A conflict between the hero and any other dream character suggests a basic disharmony between two facets of our own character. The hero often appears in dreams as an antidote to some hated external figure within the dreamer's everyday life.

High Priest/Astrologer or other person with esoteric knowledge

The higher self often presents itself in dreams as a character who appears to have knowledge of magical practices or similar types of knowledge. it is as though we can only become aware of this deeper knowledge by meeting our teacher first.

Hill/Mound

To be on top of a hill indicates we are aware of our own expanded vision. We have worked hard to achieve something and are able to survey and assess the results of what we have done. To be climbing a hill in the company of others often indicates that we have a common goal – that a journey we thought was ours alone is actually not – and we can use their knowledge to help us. To dream that we are going downhill would indicate we are feeling as if circumstances are pushing us in a certain direction.

Hole

A hole usually represents a difficult situation. If we are falling into a hole then we are getting into the unconscious side of our fears, that is, getting beneath the surface of our personalities. A hole above our heads can signify a way through to spiritual understanding. On a different level, a round hole represents the Heavens; a square hole represents the Earth.

Holiday

To be on holiday in a dream indicates a sense of relaxation and of satisfying one's own needs without having to take care of others. It could also be a warning that it is time to take a break from everyday life.

Hollow

Dreaming of feeling hollow connects with our feelings of emptiness, lack of purpose, direction and control in our lives. We may also be lacking motivation. To dream of being in a hollow would indicate that we need some kind of protection from what is going on around us.

Home

The home, and particularly the parental home, can stand for shelter, warmth and nourishment. To dream of being at home signifies a return to the standards we learnt as a child. The home can also represent sanctuary, that is a place where we can be ourselves without fear of reprisal.

Honey

Honey represents pleasure and sweetness. To dream of eating honey can be to recognise that we need to give ourselves pleasure. Equally, it can indicate the very essence of our feelings. Honey has links to fertility and virility. So, in a dream this would indicate that we are perhaps entering a much more actively sexual or fertile time.

Hood

A hood has a menacing air to it and it may indicate that there is a part of us that feels threatened in some way. More likely is the idea that part of our personality may be invisible to us and needs to be uncovered in order for us to function. Traditional interpretation said that for a woman to be wearing a hood indicated she was being deceitful. If a man is wearing a hood, it suggests that he is withdrawing from a situation.

Hook

When we dream of a hook we are understanding that, we have an ability to draw things towards us that are either good or bad. It can also indicate that we are being 'hooked', and therefore not being allowed the freedom we want. In childhood dreams the hook can represent the hold that a parent has over us. This symbolism can continue into adulthood, depicting the way that we allow people to take control within our lives.

Horns – *see* **Antlers**

Horse
The figure of a horse in dreams represents the vitality present in the dreamer. Traditionally a white horse describes the state of their spiritual awareness; a brown one the more rational and sensible side, while a black horse is the passionate side of the dreamer's nature. A pale horse suggests death, and a winged horse depicts the soul's ability to transcend the earthly plane. If the horse is under strain or dying there may be a problem with motivation and there may be insurmountable pressure in the life of the dreamer. When the horse is being harnessed the dreamer may be focusing too hard on thoroughly practical objectives. In a man's dream, a mare will denote the Anima, a woman, or the realm of the feminine. In a woman's dream, if she is being kicked by a horse, this may indicate her own Animus or her relationship with a man. A horse that can get through any door and batter down all obstacles is a representation of the collective Shadow – those aspects of the personality which most people attempt to suppress. The horse as a beast of burden often signifies the mother archetype. In modern dreams the car has largely taken over from the horse as a symbol with many of the same associations.

Horseshoe
The horseshoe is a lucky symbol and, traditionally, if it is turned upwards it represents the moon and protection from evil. When turned downwards the power is reputed to 'drain out', bringing bad luck. The horseshoe is also connected as a lucky symbol to weddings. Traditionally, to dream of a horseshoe may indicate that there will shortly be a wedding in your family or peer group.

Hospital – *see also* **Operation**
Depending on our attitude to hospitals, when one appears in a dream it can either represent a place of safety, or a place where one's very being is

threatened and we become vulnerable. It can also represent that aspect within ourselves that knows when some kind of respite is needed, possibly in order to re-evaluate a situation.

Hot

Good feelings can be translated in dreams to a physical feeling. To dream of being hot indicates warm, passionate feelings. To be aware that our surroundings are hot indicates that we are loved and cared for. Now and again, extreme emotion can be interpreted as a physical feeling – so anger, jealousy or other such feelings can be experienced as heat. Experiencing something as hot that should be cold indicates that we are perhaps having difficulty in sorting out our feelings.

Hotel

If a hotel crops up in dreams, then we may need to escape from a situation for a while. Alternatively, it may be that our current situation is of a temporary nature or shows that we may be aware of our own insecurities and may not feel particularly grounded.

Living in a hotel often signifies a basic restlessness and unsettled aspect of the dreamer's character. The dreamer may be attempting to escape from himself.

House

A house nearly always refers to the soul and the manner in which we set up our lives. If we are initially aware that the house is not empty – that there is something in it (e.g. furnishings) – it indicates some aspect of the dreamer which needs to be considered. There being someone else in the house may mean that the dreamer is feeling threatened by an aspect of his own personality. If there are different activities going on, this suggests antagonism between two parts of our personality, possibly the creative and the intellectual, or the logical and intuitive. The front of the house portrays the facade we present to the outside world. Going into or out of the house means we are in a position to decide whether we need at that time to be more introverted or extroverted. Being outside the house depicts the more public side of ourselves. In a dream of an impressive, awe-inspiring house we are conscious of the Self or the Soul, the 'higher' aspects of ourselves. Moving to a larger house implies that there is need for a change in our lives, perhaps to achieve a more open way of life, or even for more emotional space. If a small house is seen the dreamer is seeking security, or perhaps the safety of babyhood, without responsibility. If the smallness of the house is constricting the dreamer may be being trapped by responsibilities, and may need to escape. Work on the house, cementing, repairing, and making changes, shows that relationships may need to be worked on or repaired, or perhaps we need to look at health matters. We may need to take note of the damage or decay that has occurred in our lives.

The different rooms and parts of houses in dreams indicate the diverse aspects of one's personality and experience. For example:

Attic Dreaming of being in an attic is to do with past experiences and old memories. Interestingly, it can highlight family patterns of behaviour and attitudes which have been handed down.

Basement/cellar The cellar most often represents the subconscious and those things we may have suppressed through an inability to handle them. A basement can also highlight the power that is available to us provided we are willing to make use of it. We may not have come to terms with our own sexuality and prefer to keep it hidden. It can also represent family beliefs and habits, particularly those that we have internalised without realising it.

Bathroom In dreams our attitude to personal cleanliness and our most private thoughts and actions can be shown as the bathroom or toilet.

Bedroom The bedroom portrays a place of safety where we can relax and be as sensual as we wish.

Hall The hallway in a dream is representative of how we meet and relate to other people, though it is also indicative of how we make the transition from the private to the public self and vice versa.

Kitchen Being the 'heart' of the house, this shows how we nurture and care for others.

Hunger

Apart from the dreamer actually being hungry, to experience hunger in a dream suggests that our physical, emotional or mental needs are not being properly satisfied – every human being has needs that require fulfilment.

Hunt

Dreaming of being hunted is mostly taken to be to do with one's sexuality. Its even older meaning is linked with death, particularly a death containing an aspect of ritual killing or sacrifice. By association, therefore, to dream of a hunt is to register the necessity for a change of state in everyday life.

Hurricane

When we experience a hurricane in a dream, we are sensing the force of an element in our lives that is beyond our control. A hurricane can also be symbolic of our passion – we may need to figure if we can control it – with the consequences for others being of importance.

Icon – *see* **Religious Imagery**

Illness – *see also* **Sickness**
Dreaming of illness may alert us to the fact that all is not well either with ourselves or our immediate environment. We are perhaps not putting ourselves in touch with a force that can help us. The nature of the illness may give some indication as to what is amiss, or it may highlight what needs to be done in order to make a situation improve.

Imitation
To dream of being imitated can mean that we are aware that whatever we have done is the correct thing to do and that other people can learn from our example. It can equally mean that other people are seeing us as being leaders, when we ourselves do not necessarily feel that it is the correct role for us. Imitating someone else suggests we are aware of their greater knowledge and wisdom.

Immersion
To be immersed in water indicates the way we handle our emotions. We could be trying to find that part of us that is forever innocent. We are attempting to clarify situations, ideas and attitudes that have been suggested to us by other people.

To be immersed in something, that is in the sense of being focused, reveals we need to concentrate on one thing only in order to understand ourselves.

Immobility
To be made immobile in a dream is to suggest that either the energy has run out of a particular situation, or that circumstances around us are trapping us.

Imp

An imp appearing in a dream usually indicates disorder and difficulty. The imp often has the same significance as the Devil in tormenting us, creating difficulty and harming us. The imp can also represent the uncontrolled negative part of ourselves, that part that instinctively creates chaos and takes great joy in doing so. It is perhaps an aspect of loss of control.

Incense – *see* **Religious Imagery**

Incest – *see also* **Sex**

Incest is such a taboo subject that to dream of it seldom refers to the physical act. It usually represents the need and desire we have to be in control. It is possible that incest in real life occurs because the child has not yet been allowed to sort out his or her feelings so far as the family are concerned. Since self-image and sexuality are so closely connected, incest in dreams is much more likely to be an effort to sort out our feelings about ourselves.

Income

The income we earn is an important part of our everyday structure, so any dream connected with this will tend to signify our attitude towards our wants and needs. To dream of an increased income shows we feel we have overcome some obstacle in ourselves and can accept that we have value. A drop in income signifies our neediness, and perhaps our attitude to poverty. Dreaming of receiving a private income suggests we perhaps need to look at our relationships with other people.

Infection

Dreaming of having an infection suggests that there is the possibility of us having internalised negative attitudes from other people. However, it greatly depends on which part of our body we see as infected. If, for example, the leg is infected, then this will denote we are being held up somehow. It may also be that we are being negatively influenced.

Initiation – *see* **Religious Imagery**

Injection

If we are given an injection, then we are feeling as though our space has been penetrated. To dream of giving an injection suggests that we are attempting to force ourselves on other people – this may have sexual connotations. An injection may also be our way of healing, thus making ourselves better. More negatively, an injection can indicate short term pleasure rather than long term gain.

Insects

Insects in dreams can reflect the feeling that something is bugging us – something we could do without. It may also indicate a feeling of insignificance and powerlessness. It will depend on the particular insect in the dream as to the interpretation. Thus, a wasp might indicate danger, whereas a beetle could mean either dirt or protection. More positively, insects can appear in dreams as reminders of instinctive behaviour.

Intestines – *see* Body

Intoxication

When we are intoxicated in a dream it can be important to decide why we are so. Being drunk can indicate a loss of control, whereas a change of state brought about by drugs can represent a change in awareness. The changes that occur in consciousness through intoxication can be mirrored in a dream. Sometimes that change can be depressive – suggesting a need to explore the negative in our lives; sometimes they can be euphoric – showing our ability to reach a state similar to a kind of mania.

Intruder

The intruder in a woman's dream often represents an image of her own inner masculinity, i.e. the Animus. In a man's dream an intruder often personifies the shadow. Through a change in the dreamer's attitude it is possible to bring about a much better and more meaningful relationship with himself.

Iris – *see* Flowers

Iron

When iron appears in dreams, it usually represents our strengths and determination. It can perhaps also signify the rigidity of our emotions or beliefs. When we dream of using a clothes iron we are often attempting to make ourselves more presentable. We may also be trying to 'smooth things over'. Iron in a dream can also signify the part of ourselves that requires discipline.

Island

Dreaming of an island signifies the loneliness one can go through. An island can also represent safety in that, by isolating ourselves, we are not subject to external demands. Occasionally we all need to recharge our batteries, and to dream of an island can help, or warn, us to do this, which will in turn help us to function better. On another plane, an island can signify a retreat – somewhere that is cut off from the world – which will allow us to contemplate our inner self.

Ivy

Dreaming of ivy denotes, on one level, celebration and fun. However, it can symbolise the clinging dependence that can develop within relationships. Because ivy has the symbolism of constant affection, we can recognise that we are in need of love and affection. On yet another level, ivy symbolises immortality and eternal life.

Jackal

Esoterically, the jackal is the servant of the transformer, guiding souls from the earth plane into the light. It is often associated with the graveyard, and therefore with death.

Jade

This is an extremely potent image in Chinese dream interpretation. As the jewel of heaven it is a symbol of sincerity and, in various forms, suggest intellect, benevolence, humility and chastity. It always symbolises good fortune.

Jailer

A jailer in a dream can suggest a strong sense of restriction either by some part of our personality or by an external force. There may arise a period of loneliness and a sense of being trapped in an ongoing situation. The spiritual side of one's nature may give us the ability to break out of the situation, or bring us to a realisation that we must remain within the particular situation for the time being.

Jar

In old style symbolism a jar, or any kind of hollow container, represents womanhood. For a woman it can represent her ability to be a mother and in a man it can represent the principle of 'mothering'. On a slightly more esoteric note a jar can suggest the more sensitive side of our nature, so being jarred or shaken up represents being hurt by what is happening. If the jar is broken one has received some deep hurt.

Jewels – *see also* **Necklace**

Dreaming about jewels almost always means those things that we value most. These could be personal qualities, such as our integrity, our being ourselves, or perhaps even our essential being. When we feel we know what we are looking for, we are somehow aware of its value to others. Looking for jewels up a mountain or in a cave symbolise our attempt to find those parts of ourselves that may be valuable in the future. Counting jewels may mean that a time of reflection is needed. From a spiritual point of view jewels and their understanding can enhance personal development. Many stones also have healing properties.

Judge/Justice – *see also* Authority Figures *and* Jury

Often when we are attempting to stabilise two different states or ways of being, the figure of justice or balance can appear within a dream. This is to warn us that we may need to use both the physical and spiritual aspects of ourselves successfully. Since justice is usually to do with the correct way to do things according to group belief, we may feel that there is the need to conform with others or that we are doing, or are about to do, something which goes against the grain.

Judgement

Being able to use judgement, whether good or otherwise, is a skill which comes with maturity. In dreams we may find ourselves making the types of judgement which we would not normally do in waking life. For instance, we may pride ourselves on not being at all judgemental and find that, in dreams, that part of ourselves which judges behaviour works in a completely differently way.

Jungle

A jungle can often represent chaos. This chaos can be either positive or negative, depending on other elements in the dream, and may suggest some kind of obstacle or barrier that has to be passed through in order to reach a new state of understanding. Being trapped in a jungle suggests we may be trapped by negative and frightening feelings from the unconscious, though having come through a jungle would indicate that we have passed through, and overcome, aspects of our lives which we have previously found difficult. In mythology and fairy tales, cutting through the jungle often represents overcoming the impenetrable defences created by feminine awareness.

Jumping

The act of jumping can be somewhat ambiguous in a dream. Repetitive movement usually suggests the need to look at what we are doing and perhaps to express ourselves in a different way. Jumping up can indicate reaching for something that is above us, beyond our reach and requires effort to achieve, whilst jumping down can mean exploring the unconscious or those parts of ourselves which we have not yet examined. Jumping up and down can indicate frustration or joy.

Jury

A group of people in dreams sitting in judgement suggests that we are having to deal either with issues of peer pressure, that is how others think of us, or with our own estimation of ourselves. We may be questioning the values which we have adopted, or feel that we or a part of us have not been true to our own ideals – we have been found wanting. Being a member of a jury calls into question our ability to belong to a group of like-minded people or not. For example, we may not feel we can go along with the group decision. Provided we adhere to our own inner truth, we cannot be judged.

Kaleidoscope

A child is fascinated by the patterns that a kaleidoscope creates – no two being the same and yet each one being regular in its repetition and reflection within itself. The dream image of a kaleidoscope can introduce us to our own creativity, which may have become trapped. It connects us with our childlike selves, and with the beauty of basic patterns such as the mandala and the intricacies of creativity. We become aware of our own 'smallness' within the larger scheme of things.

Kangaroo

This animal often stands for motherhood, and also strength.

Kettle – *see also* Cauldron

A kettle is often taken to symbolise transformation and change. In dreams it will have an almost magical significance and indicate practical, pragmatic learning to do with the process of change. In some instances, like all hollow objects, a kettle can represent femininity and transformation.

Key/Keyhole – *see also* Lock *and* Prison

A key has obvious significance in that it locks or unlocks that which needs opening or closing. This may be one's potential or perhaps old memories, experiences or emotions. For instance, if the key opens a door something will be revealed – usually to our advantage, whereas if it locks the door we are trying to shut something away, perhaps the past or situations we do not wish to handle. Keys often appear in dreams. To dream of a bunch of keys suggests the need to 'open up' the whole of our personalities to new experiences. Sometimes the materialor design of the key will be significant. The more mundane, the more mundane is the solution.

We hold within us many of the answers to our difficulties, but often need a down-to-earth worldly symbol to trigger off our ability to work out solutions we have previously hidden. Silver and gold keys represent – respectively – transient and spiritual power.

Peering through a keyhole suggests that our vision and understanding is restricted in some way, or that we are being excluded from activity. Being unable to fit a key into a keyhole indicates inappropriate behaviour. If the size of keyhole is wrong, we have the choice of adjusting, in waking life, our knowledge (represented by the key) or the way we apply that knowledge (the keyhole). Noticing that there is no keyhole indicates a problem in reconciling one's inner and outer self. Conventionally, the keyhole has been taken to represent the feminine, more sensitive side of our personality.

Kidnap

Within any situation we can find that our own fears and doubts cause us to be victims at various times in our lives. Being kidnapped in a dream highlights our ability to be taken over and forced to do, or be, something against our will. To be the kidnapper shows that we are trying to influence someone else and need to moderate our actions.

Kidneys – *see* Body

Killing

Killing is an extreme answer to a problem. It indicates the violent ending to a predicament. Killing someone in a dream is attempting to be rid of the power they have over us. Dreaming of being killed suggests that factors with which the dreamer is dealing are making him, or a part of him, ineffective in everyday life.

King

A king surfacing in a dream usually represents the father or father figure. An emperor may indicate that some of the father's attitudes are alien to the dreamer, but should perhaps be accepted. When the king is old or on the point of dying the dreamer will be able to discard old or outdated family values.

Kissing

Kissing someone in a dream usually suggests acceptance, approval or respect. Dreaming of kissing someone whom we do not like in real life may indicate having to come to terms with qualities within ourselves which we actively dislike in others. Kissing also suggests that we are sealing a pact, or coming to an understanding. Being kissed on the forehead indicates a lack of sexual involvement and counts more as a blessing.

Kitchen

In dreams, the kitchen can often represent the mother, or rather the mothering function, highlighting the nurturing aspect. The kitchen is the place from which we go out into the world, and to which we return. It is also the place in which transformation can take place. Even in today's climate of convenienve foods, there is still the sense of work in the kitchen being an offering.

Kite

The kite represents freedom, particularly freedom from responsibility, but at the same time suggests that our activities should have an element of control about them. The expertise needed to fly a kite is only learnt through experience. In Chinese lore, the kite symbolised the wind and can suggest ones spiritual aspirations.

Knee – *see* Body

Kneeling

Kneeling usually suggests submission or sometimes supplication. Initially, kneeling represented giving someone or something status in our lives – that is, putting ourselves on a lower level. In dreams, this is the most frequent explanation. If kneeling is a way of being in contact with the earth it indicates a need to be in contact with the basic aspects of life.

Knife

A cutting implement in a dream usually signifies some kind of severance, whether from a person, relationship or situation. We may need to cut out what is non essential. It can be important in a dream about a knife to notice what type is being used, and what the action is. A stabbing action suggests penetration, whereas a slashing action suggests the violent removal of unwanted material. In a woman's dream this is probably more to do with her own fear of penetration and violation, whereas in a man's dream it is highlighting his own aggression.

Knight

It will depend whether the knight appears in a woman's or a man's dream as to the most relevant interpretation. There is the standard interpretation for the female, that of the knight in shining armour, and therefore a romantic relationship – a search for the perfect partner. A man may be looking for the heroic part of himself; the part that will take risks because they are there to be taken. In both cases the knight may represent the spiritual side of one's nature. A 'black' knight is often taken as a figure of evil, whereas a 'white' knight is a fighter for the good of all. Psychologically, the knight in a dream signifies the guiding principle.

Knob

There are many interpretations which can be given for a knob. Just as a key can represent an answer to a problem, so also can a knob suggest a particular course of action for the dreamer. This may be a turning point in one's life, a new way of accessing information or a different way of regarding the situation. Not being able to turn a doorknob can suggest an obstacle which stands in our way. In some dreams the knob will represent the penis or masculine principle.

Knot

A simple knot seen in a dream could represent a blockage in the natural flow of events or the need to take a different direction in a project. To be untying a knot suggests solving a problem which is more complex than we first appreciated, and which may take time to undo. In more symbolic terms, a knot can suggest a maze or labyrinth which itself represents the complex feminine make-up. A more complex knot could indicate that we are bound to a situation by a sense of duty or guilt. To be feeling knotted up inside suggests being under some emotional strain.

L

Label
A label is a means of identification, of establishing one's right to own some object or of differentiating between several different categories. Dreams can often highlight basic human instincts and our sense of identity is one of the most important instincts we have. To be able to label or mark our possessions in some fashion gives us a place in the world, a right to belong, to mark up our successes or failures. To be re-labelling something suggests that we have rectified a misperception.

Labour
'Hard labour' suggests self flagellation or self punishment in what we are doing. However, if a woman dreams of being in labour she perhaps has an issue with her wish and desire to be pregnant, or with that of mothering. It may also be that she is bringing a scheme or project to fruition, and is about to achieve a long cherished goal.

Laboratory
Dreaming of a laboratory indicates we need to make an impartial appraisal of what is happening to us. If we are specimens in a laboratory we may feel that we are being judged in some fashion, whereas being the scientist or technician suggests that we may need to look more carefully at the situation highlighted by the dream. Being in a laboratory suggests a more objective approach to life, and often seems to be a feature of dreams about alien beings.

Labyrinth – *see also* **Maze**
In undertaking our own journey of discovery and exploring our deeper personality, we open ourselves up to all sorts of potentials, some of which will lead us to new experiences and some of which will lead us into cul-de -sacs. It is often at this point that we dream of exploring a

labyrinth or a series of underground interlinking passages. Often such a dream will force us into confronting our own fears and doubts, and overcoming the Shadow, or that part we most dread and have difficulty in understanding. The labyrinth is also the representation of the hidden feminine mysterious part of our personality.

Ladder

The ladder often represents our ability to move from one phase of existence to another and denotes how secure we feel in moving from one situation to another. Such a dream may occur during career changes and can signify promotion. Probably the most well known ladder dream is the 'Jacob's Ladder' one recounted in the Bible. This signifies the transition between earth and heaven, and in this context the ladder shows the ability to move from the physical realms of existence into an awareness of the spiritual dimension in life. In spiritual development such a dream is fairly commonplace.

Lagoon/Lake

The unconscious side of ourselves – an abundant source of power when it can be properly accessed and understood – often manifests in dreams as a lake or lagoon. The home of the darker, more occult side of femininity and sensitivity – as seen in the Arthurian legends – the lagoon appears in dreams as we come to terms with this side of ourselves. The lagoon as part of a wider sea is also a potent symbol of deep emotion.

Lame/Lameness

A loss of confidence and strength suggests that part of our personality is not functioning correctly. This will often manifest in dreams as lameness. As we become more proficient in interpretation, lameness on the left side will show difficulty with the softer sensitive feminine whilst on the right it will suggest problems with the masculine assertive side of the personality. In mythological terms, lameness is taken to represent the imperfections of the physical realms which are a necessary part of existence.

Lance

Any type of lance, being both a cutting and penetrative instrument, has the same meaning in dreams as a knife. It suggests masculine power and therefore sometimes the sexual act. Lancing a boil or cutting out bad flesh creates a sense of releasing negative energy or contamination.

Large – *see* Size

Late
Being aware of being late in a dream suggests that we are not totally in control of the situations around us. Psychologically, such a dream is said to represent the search for perfection and the feeling that we have, or may be will, let someone down. If someone else is late in a dream, we may be conscious that there is a lack of communication in some way.

Laugh/Laughter
Laughter in the spiritual sense signifies pure joy. If we ourselves are laughing we may be experiencing a release of tension. Often the object of our entertainment will give a clue to the bearing of the dream on everyday life. Being laughed at in dreams suggests we may have a fear of being ridiculed, or may have done something which we feel is not appropriate.

Lavatory – *see* Toilet

Lead (Metal)
The conventional explanation of lead appearing in a dream is that we have a situation around us which is a burden to us. It can indicate that the time is ripe for transformation and transmutation. In spiritual symbolism lead stands for bodily consciousness, and has connotations with the process of alchemy, of the transformation of the base into the pure.

Lead and Leading
Leadership qualities are not necessarily ones that everybody will use. Often we can surprise ourselves in dreams by doing things that we would not normally do, and taking the lead is one of them. This suggests taking control of a situation around us. Leading someone in a dream pre-supposes that we know what we are doing and where we are going. Being

led indicates that we have allowed someone else to take control of a situation around us. Dreaming of a dog lead would symbolise the connection between ourselves and our lesser nature, and the necessity to introduce some kind of controlling element into our lives.

Leaf/Leaves

A leaf often represents a period of growth and fertility and can also indicate time. It will depend on the look of the leaves as to how they are interpreted. For instance bright green leaves can suggest hope and new opportunities. Dead leaves signify a period of sadness or barrenness.

Leak

Dreaming of a leak suggests we are wasting or losing energy in some way, and may indicate that we are being careless with our personal resources. Someone may be draining us emotionally and we need to be more responsible in our actions.

Left

The left-side suggests the less controlling, the more receptive side. Often it is taken to represent all that is dark and sinister and instinctive, and those parts of our personality we do our best to curb. It is connected with what is experienced as good inside and with personal behaviour, without attention to any code of conduct. It is sympathetic in expression, and understanding by nature, so anything appearing on the left-side in dreams can be accepted as evidence of support. Any pain experienced on the left-side is interpreted in terms of sensitivity. It also expresses the more feminine attributes. Feelings of being left behind suggest a sense of inferiority, and of having to leave the past behind.

Leg – *see* Body

Lending

In spiritual terms, the concept of lending is connected with healing and support. If in a dream we are lending an object to someone we are aware that the characteristic that object represents can only be given away temporarily. If someone is lending us an article then we are perhaps not responsible enough to possess what it represents on a full time basis. Conversely, we may only need it for a short time. If we are being lent money we need to look at the way we are managing our resources, but also at what guidance or support we need to do this. If we are lending money, we are creating an obligation within our lives.

Leopard
The leopard represents oppression and aggression and traditionally the underhandedness of power wrongly used.

Leper
Spiritually, a leper in a dream can suggest that we are having to deal with a moral dilemma which takes us away from compassion and caring. We may feel that our lives have been contaminated, or that we have been rejected by the society in which we live, or that conversely we are having to accept or reject some kind of impurity in others. It will depend on the rest of the dream which interpretation is correct.

Letter – *see also* **Address** *and* **Parcel**
At its simplest, a letter suggests communication of some sort. An official letter may represent information we need or have, a bill may indicate that some action we propose to take has a cost, while a love letter may mean that we are aware of how much we are cared about by others. If we are sending a letter we need to be clear about our own way of communicating.

Library
A library in a dream can often represent the sum total of our life's experience. It suggests both the wisdom and skills that we ourselves have accumulated, and the collected wisdom available to all humanity. It can also represent our intellectual capacity and the way we handle knowledge. Additionally, in those who have, or are developing, clairvoyance it is often taken as the Akashic records – the spiritual records of existence.

Lift
A lift usually indicates how we deal with information. For instance, a lift going down would suggest going down into the subconscious, while a lift

going up would be moving towards the spiritual. It is believed that in the sleep state we leave our bodies, and this can be reflected in dreams of lifts or elevators. Thus, descending in a lift and getting stuck represents the entrapment of the spiritual by the physical body, and going up in a lift and getting stuck can suggest that we are too geared towards the material world.

Light
Any kind of light in a dream usually means illumination. It is much to do with confidence. In dreams it is often the quality of the light which is important. For instance, a bright light suggests intuition whereas a dim light might suggest the potential for sickness. To feel lighter signifies we are feeling better about ourselves. A lamp in dreams often signifies guidance, and wisdom, particularly from a divine source. An old fashioned lamp will represent ancient wisdom, often of a personal kind rather than universal. A candle is often used in meditational practices, and therefore in dreaming becomes an archetypal symbol of the soul.

Lighthouse
Spiritually a lighthouse highlights the correct course of action to help us achieve our spiritual goals. It can act as a shaft of light which can lead us into calmer waters. A lighthouse is a warning system, and in dreams it tends to warn us of emotional difficulties.

Lightning
Lightning in a dream reveals unexpected changes, often occurring through some type of sudden realisation of a personal truth, or of a more universal awareness. It can also indicate a revelation which knocks away the structures we have carefully built in as safeguards in our lives. There is often a discharge of tension or passion, which may initially seem destructive, but ultimately clears away the debris of outmoded ideas and principles. Lightning can also in the more spiritual sense suggest the Holy Spirit.

Lily
Spiritually lilies are a symbol of resurrection and of everlasting life.

Because of their association with funerals for many, lilies can signify death. They can, however, also symbolise purity (and hence virginity), nobility, grace, and other aspects of femininity.

Lion

A lion lying with a lamb suggest that there is a union, or compatibility of opposites; instinct and spirit going hand in hand. The lion stands for dignity, strength and courage. It can also represent the ego and the feelings associated with it. If in the dream there is a struggle with the lion there should be a successful development as long as the dreamer is not overpowered or the lion killed.

Liquid

One of the symbols of liquid is to do with liquidity – that is, having resources or equity which can be realised in order to be used effectively. This can be on either a physical or emotional level. Liquid in dreams can have more than one meaning. Water has its own meaning, but other liquids will lend themselves to different interpretation. Orange juice, for instance, might suggest looking at matters of health. Because liquid is always connected with 'flow' the idea of allowing feelings to flow properly is one which needs to be considered. A strong symbol in spiritual development is golden liquid, which can represent both power and energy.

Liver – *see* **Body**

Lock, locked – *see also* **Key** *and* **Prison**

A lock appearing in a dream may highlight the need to free up whatever we have shut away in, or from, our lives. To be forcing a lock would indicate that we perhaps need to work against our own inclinations to lock things away in order to be free of inhibitions. We may also be trying to bring about a situation which requires a good deal of force or energy in order to succeed. To recognise in a dream that a part of our body has become locked suggests that we are carrying extreme tension. It is possible that we need to release that tension in a physical way in order to be healthy.

Loom

The loom in spiritual terms suggests fate, time, and the weaving of destiny. It symbolises creativity, whether more mechanical or craft-oriented, and signifies the ability to create our lives according to a set pattern.

Lorry/Commercial vehicle

A lorry in a dream will mean the same as a car, except that the drives and ambitions will be linked more with work and how we relate on a business basis to the outside world.

Lost

The search for the lost object or the lost chord (in the sense of a missing vibration) epitomises the search for enlightenment. To have lost something in a dream may mean that we have forgotten, or are out of touch with, matters which could be important. To have suffered some kind of loss or deprivation may mean that part of ourselves or our lives is now dead or defunct and we must learn to cope without it. This may be an opportunity, a friend or a way of thought which has previously sustained us. We may have lost the ability or the motivation to make clear decisions and must remain in a state of confusion. Often this type of dream is classified as an anxiety dream.

Lottery

Nowadays the lottery has a great deal of significance in people's lives. It is a sort of legitimised gambling or taking of risks, and in dreams epitomises the achievement of all that one could wish for. It also signifies the principle of luck operating on one's behalf. Rather than the effort we are prepared to put in to gain some kind of profit, we instinctively recognise the element of chance or happenstance in our lives. A lottery ticket suggests the recording of our desires. Spiritually the lottery represents the ability to take chances, to rely on fate rather than good judgement.

Low

'Feeling low' can suggest inadequacy or depression. To 'be below' can denote a need to explore the negativity of a relationship.

Machine

Machinery in dreams often focuses on the mechanical processes within our bodies which enable us to survive. These functions are those associated with the automatic nervous system which continue with the minimum of maintenance.

Machines can also suggest a mechanistic way of looking at life, of creating a universe which meshes together but without the back up of a creative process. Perceiving a large machine such as a tank in dreams can suggest an unstoppable force.

Maggots

Maggots in dreams may reflect our own fears about death and illness, but can also suggest impurities within the body or within a situation around us. For most people maggots cause such a reaction of distaste that they will tend to represent something that we cannot 'handle'.

Magic

Magic in dreams speaks of our ability to link with our deepest powers. They can be the powers of sexuality or the powers of control, or of power over our surroundings. We are all intrigued by mystery or the inexplicable, and have the need to make things happen – a symbol to do with magic can alert us to our own inner talents.

Magistrate – *see* Authority Figures

Magnet

The magnet has the ability to create a 'field' round itself, a field of magnetic energy. This energy is similar to the energy field that clairvoyants and psychics perceive around other people, and often a magnet appearing in a dream alerts us to the intrinsic power that we have, which seems to be inert until such times as it is activated by greater knowledge We all have within us the ability to attract or repel others, and often a magnet appearing in a dream will highlight that ability. Since of itself the magnet is inert, it is the power it has that is important. We often need to realise that the influence that we have over other people comes not only from ourselves, but also from our interaction with them.

Magnifying glass
When anything is magnified in a dream it is being brought to our attention. To be using a magnifying glass indicates that we should be paying attention to the details of our lives. We should be able to act in full awareness of what we are doing – making what we are looking at conscious. When the magnifying glass itself and not what we are looking at is important, we are recognising our own abilities, our own power within a situation.

Magpie/Jackdaw
Because of the belief that magpies and jackdaws are thieves, to dream of one may indicate that a someone is trying to take away something of value. The magpie can denote good news.

Make-up
To be aware of make-up in dreams is to acknowledge that we have a choice as to the sort of person we want to be. We can choose the image we wish to project, and can create whatever facade we choose. Our use of make-up in dreams may depend on how we use it in everyday life. It can be used to create beauty or to cover up imperfections.

Man
Any masculine figure which appears in a dream demonstrates an aspect or facet of the dreamer's personality so that we can recognise it. There is a particular group of behaviour patterns within each of us that makes us recognisable. In dreams these patterns and characteristics can be magnified so that they are easily identifiable – they can often appear as personalities. Much energy and power can become available once their significance is understood. A man in a dream can identify the Shadow

(the negative side of himself) for a man, and the Animus for a woman. Even when we are threatened by a negative character trait, we still have the ability to access room for improvement.

An older man (if the man is white-haired or holy) can represent the innate wisdom we all have. Such a person can also signify the father in dreams.

A large man appearing in our dreams indicates either our appreciation of the strengths, certainties and protection which our basic beliefs give us or, if we feel intimidated, suggests that we may be threatened or made apprehensive by those very qualities.

A man in woman's dream highlights the more logical side of her nature. She has, or can develop, all the aspects of the masculine which enable her to function with success in the external world. If the man is one she knows or loves she may be trying to understand her relationship with him.

An unknown man is generally that part of the dreamer's personality which is not recognised. In a woman's dream it may be the masculine side of herself, and in a man's dream it is The Self.

Mantis

The Mantis, as with most insects, can often show the trickster part of us that can create problems when things are effectively working out for us. We may be the trickster or perhaps we are the one being tricked. This is usually on an emotional level and, by and large, if the dreamers are completely honest they will know the genuine meaning of the dream.

Manure

Some of the experiences which we have to go through can be distressing or difficult. If we cannot understand what is going on and do not utilise it as part of the development we all go through, those experiences remain with us and cause difficulty later on. These bad experiences may appear within a dream as manure ready to be dealt with by natural processes.

Map

A map in dreams can represent the help we need in our quest to find the way forward. It often indicates the clarification of the direction we should be taking in life. It is worth remembering that we need to read the map ourselves, and therefore we are our own guides. Not being able to read a map might indicate confusion, whilst knowing we needed a map but not having one might suggest a lack of necessary information.

Mare – *see* **Horse**

Marigold – *see* **Flowers**

Market/Marketplace

A market complete with stalls tends to be somewhat impermanent or temporary and can be interpreted in dreams as such. It can also suggest that we need to become more commercial in the work that we are doing, or perhaps to be more creatively influenced, rather than doing something purely and simply because it is commercial. A marketplace can be viewed as a place of spiritual exchange. The stock market or a scene associated with it suggests that we probably need to pay attention to the way we handle our resources, financial or otherwise.

Marriage/Wedding

On a subliminal level we are always looking for someone to provide or enhance qualities which are not present within us, so to dream of a wedding can give an indication of the potential for growth by uniting for instance drive and receptivity. These need to come together in order to create a more effective personality. Such a dream can also give an indication as to how the dreamer views relationships and commitment.

Marsh

Dreaming of marshy ground very often represents difficulty on an emotional level. It may be hard to feel secure and properly grounded in the middle of these problems. It may be that we lack either the self-confidence or emotional support that we need to move forward. Literally there is some way in which we are feeling 'bogged down'.

Martyr

Dreaming of being a martyr suggests that there is the potential for the dreamer to turn him or her self into some kind of sacrificial victim, perhaps doing things out of a sense of duty rather than love. Not feeling that one can refuse to fulfil what others expect of us – or rather what we think they expect – can lead to the type of behaviour that may be seen, for instance, in the over possessive mother who expects her children for lunch, but then grumbles because she spends all morning cooking. Additionally, dreaming of religious martyrs can suggest behaviour we admire or some kind of fanatical act in order to prove a point.

Mask

Dreaming of a mask often makes us aware of either our own or other people's facade – the public face. Most people are capable of concealing their true selves from other people and when it is no longer appropriate behaviour this conduct can appear in dreams as a mask. This mask can be perceived as either a positive or negative more frightening mask. In primitive cultures to wear a mask such as that of an animal gave the wearer the powers of that animal.

Mattress – *see also* **Bed** *under* **Furniture**

Similar to a bed, the mattress can suggest one's private space. To dream of a mattress indicates the feeling we have about a situation we have created in our lives, whether it is comfortable or not. Interestingly, dreaming of a mattress may also suggest the temporary nature of a relationship we have.

Maypole

The maypole in a spiritual sense is a representation of the phallic, of masculine spirituality and of life-giving energy. It is the central axis of the world that we create for ourselves; thus to dream of a maypole may have sexual connotations, but also may indicate the way in which we handle our own lives.

Maze – *see also* **Labyrinth**

A maze often represents a confusion of ideas and feelings. Psychologically, the maze in a dream may suggest the variety of opinions and authoritative beliefs that we come up against in our ordinary, everyday world, and which may represent blocks to progress. There are conflicting drives and assumptions and we often discover that in attempting to find our way through the maze we have learnt something about our own courage, our own ability to meet problems. x

Medal

Human beings appreciate feeling good about themselves. A medal being awarded in a dream acknowledges our abilities and/or successes – not just in the immediate moment – but gives a tangible reminder of what we have done.

Medicine

Sometimes an incident in waking life can be unpleasant at the time, but ultimately results in some kind of healing, and is finally good for us. In dreams medicine can stand as such a symbol. Medicine also may suggest a health problem, or a circumstance which can be changed from the negative to the positive.

Meditation

Interpreting the act of meditation will depend on whether the dreamer meditates in real life. In someone who does, it will suggest a discipline that is helpful to the dreamer, putting him or herself in touch with intuition and spiritual matters. In someone who does not, it may indicate the need to be more introverted in order to understand the necessity to be responsible for oneself.

Medium

Mediumistic aspects in a dream can represent the dreamer's wish to be in contact with those who have passed over, whether literally, or figuratively, in the sense of not being available to us. It may be that we need to have some sort of deeper contact with our own unconscious, or with the dead. Interestingly, there may be a play on words, and the middle way is called for.

Menstruation – *see also* **Blood** *under* **Body**

All that is mysterious in women can be symbolised by menstruation. It is only in a patriarchal society that such a natural process is seen as unclean.

Thus to dream of menstruation may be linking with the creative side of ourselves which can conceive new ideas and can create new and more wonderful 'children' out of simple material. Dreams of menstruation tend to occur as a woman goes through the various rites of passage associated with her life, such as puberty or the menopause, and can therefore sometimes stand as a symbol for opportunities lost.

Mermaid, Merman
Traditionally, the mermaid or merman belongs to the sea as well as being able to exist on land. This symbolically represents an ability to be deeply emotional and also practical and to need to spend some time in the dark recesses of the emotional self in order to exist within the natural world.

A merman or mermaid appearing in a dream is usually a call to integrate the material and emotional sides of ourselves, in order to function more effectively. Until these two separate parts are properly integrated, the human being cannot fully exist in either realm.

Metal
Any metal appearing in dreams represents the restrictions and constraints of the real world. Most metals have symbolic meanings, often connected with the planets and their qualities. Sun is represented by gold (masculine), the Moon by silver (feminine), Mercury by quicksilver (communication), Venus by copper (love), Mars by iron (drive or determination), Jupiter by tin (expansiveness), Saturn by lead (heaviness).

Microscope
A microscope appearing in a dream very often indicates that we need to pay attention to detail, or to be aware that some aspect of ourselves needs to be expanded in some way. Also we may need to be somewhat introspective and more objective in order to achieve a personal goal.

Milk – *see* Food

Mine
Dreaming of a mine signifies bringing the resources of the unconscious into the light of day. This is one of those symbols which can actually be

a word play. The things in the dream are 'mine'. The dreamer is able to use the potential available.

Mirror

The mirror suggests self-realisation backed up by wisdom. Dreaming of a mirror suggests concern over one's self-image. We are worried as to what others think of us, and need self-examination or reflection in order to function correctly. There may be some anxiety over ageing or health. By association it may be that our behaviour needs adjusting. Magically mirrors can be used to reflect back onto someone their past misdeeds or difficulties, and as one becomes more aware of personal magic, a mirror in a dream can assume this significance.

Miscarriage

Dreaming of a miscarriage suggests that we are conscious of the fact that something is out of order or has been brought to an end too quickly. In a woman's dream it will depend on whether she has actually suffered a miscarriage, since nowadays she may well not have given herself time to grieve for the loss of her child.

Dreaming of a miscarriage can also suggest the loss of work, a project or even a part of ourselves, and we need time to acclimatise.

Moat

A moat in dreams can be an emotional barrier or defence. It is a representation of our defences against intimacy. In dreams we often gain an insight into how we build or dig those enclosures. We can also decide what steps we need to take to remove them. Often it is condition of the water in the moat which gives us an awareness of our emotional state.

Mole

The mole is often taken to represent the powers of darkness, but can often signify the heedless perseverance and tenacity which enable the dreamer to succeed.

Money

Money in dreams represents our own personal resources – whether material or spiritual – and our potential for success. In some circumstances a dream of money can be linked with our view of our own power and our sexuality. It does not necessarily represent hard currency, but more the way in which we value ourselves and our own resources. The symbol of money appearing in dreams would suggest that we need to assess that value more carefully, and to become more aware of what is the 'cost' of our actions and desires. This is one of those symbols which can only be truly interpreted in the context of the dreamer's way of life.

Monkey

The qualities of mischief, impudence and inquisitiveness all belong to the monkey and characterise the immature, childish and arrested side of the dreamer's personality. While these are often seen as regressive tendencies, that of lively curiosity maintains a necessary lightness of spirit.

Monster

A monster in dreams usually stands for our negative relationship with ourselves and fear of our own emotions and drives. Something which we have allowed to grow out of all proportion comes back to haunt us and to highlight the frightened child within. Often by choosing to work with the dream image we can overcome the actual fear itself.

Moon – *see also* **Planets**

The Great Mother, in her guise as the darker, unknown side of Self, is symbolised by the moon, and therefore represents the unapproachable. The moon even in pagan times represented the emotional and feminine self. To dream of the moon, therefore, is to be in touch with that side of ourselves which is dark and mysterious. It is the intuition, the psychic, love and romance. Often in dreams the moon can also represent one's own mother or the relationship with her.

Moth

Just as the butterfly symbolises the emerging soul, so the moth stands for the Self, but perhaps in its darker sense. It represents the hidden transient side of our personality, the night time self and therefore sometimes the dreaming self.

Mother – *see* **Family**

Motorbike/Motorcycle
Imaging independent behaviour, blatant masculinity and daring the motorbike also can stand for the sexual act; it can also be a symbol of freedom. If the rider is a woman the motorcycle can suggest androgyny, while a Hell's Angel would suggest some kind of anarchical behaviour.

Mountain
The symbol of the mountain, as an archetypal representation of difficulties to be overcome, offers many alternatives and choices. In dream sequences it most often appears in order to symbolise an obstacle which needs to be overcome. We are able to challenge our own inadequacies and to free ourselves from fear. To reach the top is to achieve one's goal. Because the symbol of a mountain is common to meditation and dream work, it is often possible to work through with this image what our course of action needs to be.

Mourning – *see also* **Funeral** *and* **Weeping**
Psychologically, we need a period of adjustment when we have lost something, so the process of mourning is an important one in all sorts of ways. We not only mourn death but also the end of a relationship or a particular part of our lives. Since sometimes mourning or grieving is seen as inappropriate in waking life, it will often appear in dreams as a form of relief or release. Through dreams we may find that we can help ourselves to create a new beginning through our mourning for the old. Often some kind of a ritual is needed to mark the ending of an old phase.

Mouse
The mouse's quality of shyness can often be addressed in the dreamer, if it is recognised that this can arise from chaos and lack of understanding.

Mouth – *see* **Body**

Mud
Spiritually, mud represents the very basic primordial material from which

we are all formed, and the need to go 'back to basics'. Dreaming of mud suggests we are bogged down, perhaps by not having separated the practical from the emotional (earth and water). Mud can also represent past experiences, or our perception of them, which could hold us back.

Mummy – Egyptian

The Egyptian mummy symbolises death, but also preservation after death and therefore the afterlife and new beginnings. However, we may be trapped by old concepts and belief systems, from which we need to be set free. The most obvious connection between Mummy and mother is a play on words. In many ways, for full psychological health, our mother must 'die' to us, or rather, we must change our relationship with her, in order for us to survive. The Egyptian mummy in dreams can also symbolise our feelings about someone who has died.

Murder/Murderer

To be angry enough to wish to kill suggests that we are still holding some kind of childhood anger, since it is quite natural for a child to wish somebody dead. If we are trying to murder somebody else in a dream, we first need to understand what that person represents to us before recognising the violence of our own feelings.

We may be denying, or trying to control, a part of our own nature that we do not trust. We may also have feelings about other people which can only be safely expressed in dreams. If we ourselves are being murdered a part of our lives is completely out of balance and we are being destroyed by external circumstances.

Museum

A museum can represent the subconscious, that part of ourselves which we approach in an effort to understand who we are and where we came from. It can also signify the past, or old fashioned thoughts, concepts and ideas. Those things which are most interesting are worth preserving.

Music/Rhythm/Musical Instruments – *see also* Orchestra

Sacred sound has always been used in acts of worship, often to induce an altered state of consciousness, and music and rhythm are both an expression of our inner selves and of our connection with life. Music in dreams can equally represent a sensuous and sensual experience.

Musical instruments can symbolise the way we communicate with others. For instance, wind instruments tend to suggest the intellect. Percussion instruments suggest the basic rhythm of life.

Mystic Knot

Spiritually the mystic knot suggests Infinity, since it has no beginning and no end. In dreams in terms of self-development, it suggests a problem which cannot be solved by conventional means.

N

Nakedness – *see* **Nude**

Name

Hearing our own name in a dream is quite rare. We should be alerted to our own self-sense, to our own nature as well as our desire to belong. Conversely, hearing another person's name may lead us to look at what qualities they have in order to find a new aspect to ourselves: an aspect that will, hopefully, lead us to a more Essential Self, and to a more contented state of being.

Narrow

A sense of narrowness often suggests that a restriction or a limitation, possibly regarding communication, may be being placed on us. However, we need to differentiate between a negative and positive restriction; it may be that we should not be moved from our current path of finding.

Necklace

A woman who dreams of a man giving her a necklace should beware, as it was once thought to be a precursor to a marriage proposal. However, if her feelings about the dream border on anticipation it is worth noting that this is a very old interpretation open to a degree of scepticism. More seriously, a necklace can represent a deep abundance of feeling or emotion because of its often special meaning to its owner.

Needle

Dreaming of a needle can signify a healing power, through penetration. However, we must be alert to the aspect of 'needle dependency' so to speak, particularly if the needle is being used on us rather than by us. All in all, though, to dream of a needle indicates that we need to apply some sort of insight into our own being that is 'penetrative' and healing.

Nest

We should look at our emotional state with regard to our home life and our dependency on that – or maybe non dependency. A nest symbolises the safety of home life, so it is not surprising that women often dream of this prior to giving birth.

Nettle

In real life nettles are something to be avoided, so in a dream, when nettles appear, we are being warned that a prickly or difficult situation could be about to befall us and we should do our utmost to steer clear of it. Nettles can also symbolise 'wildness'. We should look at that with regard to ourselves and what constitutes wild behaviour for us through to the point of losing control. We must decide if a degree of healing or improvement can or cannot take place through this, since nettles are also a symbol of healing.

New

When, during a dream, a sense of 'newness' is felt, it usually represents new beginnings, new ways of progressing, or possibly even new relationships. It is also a time to look at how we can learn anew, or maybe even relearn old rules and evaluate from there.

Newspaper

A newspaper, in the waking world, tells us what's going on – with varying degrees of style and accuracy. Hence, in dreams, different newspapers mean different symbolism. A tabloid paper will suggest low level information. A broadsheet will invariably mean better, 'quality' advice. A Sunday paper often points to knowledge gained in, and through, rest, whereas a local rag or free newspaper symbolises that the news we need is just around the corner.

Niche

When we have found our niche, in everyday life, we feel protected and safe; therefore, in dreams we are being alerted to this and it may be that we just need to recognise where we are in life or what outside influences can help us get to where we want to be.

Night

Night is usually the time we can gather strength and relieve ourselves of the day's torment. The antithesis is one of fear and restlessness. We must rid ourselves of the latter symbolism in order to use the night as a forerunner to a 'new day' and a fresh approach. It must also be said that night can symbolise death, so we must look closely at the dream to determine whether this is so, and if it is what we can do about it. It does not have to be negative: it could be, for example, the death of a situation or relationship that will ultimately move us on.

Noose – *see also* **Hanging** *and* **Rope**

Apart from the obvious link to death and punishment, the symbolism of a noose centres around being or feeling trapped. We need to find out if we are in danger of trapping ourselves or if we are being manipulated by others into a potentially 'tight' situation. If the latter is the case, we must assert and express ourselves, as it could also be an attempt to curb self-expression.

North

The North signifies the Unknown, and hence sometimes darkness. It is spirituality within the world.

Nuclear Explosion – *see also* **Bomb**

If we have been anxious or even afraid of the future, or of change, then it is common to dream of an explosion. We may fear that things are going to change too quickly when we would prefer a more measured route. But change is imminent, and we must be ready to handle it lest another element of symbolism come into play – that of destructive energies.

Nude/Naked

Dreaming of being naked has various connotations but most revolve around self-image or self-expression and the need to be seen for what we really are, not what is projected. Nudity is also linked with innocence and, with that, the desire to be open and honest. This could tie in with the need for a new start; in effect – and bearing in mind we are born naked – a rebirth.

Numbers

When numbers are brought into focus in dreams they can have a personal and/or a symbolic significance. Often a number will turn up which has personal meaning, such as a relevant date, or the number of a house we may have lived in. Our minds will retain the significance of the number, even though we do not always consciously remember it ourselves. It is also worth noting that numbers are infinite and that mathematics is the link between man and science.

Nut

If the nut in question is of the metal variety, then this indicates a construction or reconstruction of our life in such a way that it will hold together more securely.

A nut – the edible kind – is seen as being a way of taking in wisdom, in other words, nourishment to the brain; this in turn can also feed, and thus enhance, any psychic power we may have.

Oar

An oar can be seen as a way of guiding us to our goal – but we must be aware that it takes skill and judgement. In other words, we are in control of our own destiny.

Oasis

All around the world an oasis is viewed as a place of sanctuary, where we may live forever in peace and contentment whilst receiving emotional invigoration. Our worries and anxieties should cast no shadow, until they eventually fade away into a distant blur. We then feel fully refreshed and can come together, step out, and roll with whatever life throws at us.

Oats

Oats are a crucial source of nourishment – simple and effective – and because of this oats have come to represent homeliness, warmth, comfort, and strength. The alternative symbolism surrounds sexuality – sowing our wild oats: it might be that we need to decide whether to branch out of a relationship or not, depending on our feelings at the time.

Obligation

Obligation in a dream relates to our sense of duty, usually to another person. It may transpire that we have to carry out a task that we do not want to, or have been putting off, but as the old saying goes, 'duty calls'.

Obscenity

We are more able to deal with obscene inclinations we may have via the dream state than in waking life. If in dreams we are seen to be involved in an obscene exploit, then we should be aware of how this is being kept in check; if it is being performed against us, then maybe we are being deceived or victimised.

Obsession

In waking life obsession is often dangerous, but if it comes up in dreams it may be an indication that there are anxieties that simply need working through. Obsession can also translate into repetition of actions, and it is likely that we are being encouraged, by the unconscious mind, to fully appreciate and understand a real situation.

Obstacle

In dreams, as in wakefulness, obstacles - whether the physical or emotional kind - have to be scaled, yet that is generally easier said than done. However, how we overcome obstacles in a dream is often a pointer to how we can handle such things as self-doubt and indecision in real life.

Obstacles in water, such as dams, islands and driftwood, symbolise both our conscious efforts to control the force of the water (and therefore our emotions) or difficulties which are being put in our way.

Ocean – *see* Sea

Octopus

An octopus can move around freely and in any direction at any given time, so the symbolism is straightforward. We need to be aware that we can have the same unrestricted movement in all senses – if we want it.

Offence

If in a dream we offend someone, then we need to be more aware of people's feelings. If we take offence, then we are tapping into our emotional sensitivity and its place in our everyday life. In another sense, if we are committing an offence, then we have to look at our behaviour.

Office

An office or work situation sometimes, in dreams, represents a place where we are comfortable (in a formal way). We would look at our feelings regarding work and authority and assess if this is so, and if not, what to do about it. An office scene can also point to our feelings about responsibility and the need to have or relinquish it.

Officer, Official – *see* **Authority Figures**

Oil

The specific type of oil determines what symbolism is to be applied. For example, cooking oil indicates a removal of dissension, whereas massage oil indicates an easing away of tension by love and care. Engine oil, on the other hand, highlights just that, our ability to keep our own engines in good working order.

Ointment

Ointment relates directly to the caring and healing process, that is, our ability to heal or need to be healed in some form or other. Also the preservation of our system and prevention of disease can be significant in the dream world.

Old, Ancient, Antique

In a dream, when we have a sense of things being old, it is an indication that we need to bring some past knowledge to the fore, or maybe some old wisdom or advice needs to be reassessed. If the 'oldness' takes the form of a man, then this could be a sign that we should take a look at our feelings surrounding time, and more specifically, death.

Old People

In dreams, old people can represent either our ancestors or grandparents, hence wisdom accrued from experience. If the old person is male – depending on the gender of the dreamer – he will stand for either the Self or the Animus. If female, then she will signify the Great Mother or the Anima. Father figures, or representations of the father, will often appear old as if to highlight their remoteness. A group of old people often appears in dreams. Usually this signifies the traditions and wisdom of the past – those things which are sacred to the 'tribe' or family. Older people usually stand for our parents even though the dream figures may bear no relationship to them.

Onion – *see also* **Food**

The onion is understood to be a symbol of wholeness – albeit a complex multi layered one – as our own personalities are. So if we dream of an onion it means we need to look at, and, in a manner of speaking, 'into' ourselves.

Operation – *see also* **Hospital**

To dream of an operation, particularly if it is being performed on us, is to allow ourselves to come to terms with our fear of illness and pain. It is, as well, the recognition that we need to get better, and that our need for that is greater than our fear. We may need to have something which is wrong for us cut out of our lives.

Oracle

Most people want to know what is going to happen to them in the future; they like also to be told what to do next – to an extent. So dreaming of an oracle links us with that perceptive part of ourselves, the part that knows what our next move is. More spiritually, the oracle represents Hidden Knowledge.

Orange – *see* **Colours** *and* **Fruit** *under* **Food**

Orchestra – *see also* **Music, Musical Instruments** *and* **Organ**

For us to function correctly we must work in harmony with others. Dreaming of an orchestra is a pointer to how we can bring elements together to achieve a wholeness.

We will need to orchestrate the moves, to take some degree of control, to 'conduct', which means listening and understanding as well as being listened to and understood.

Ore

Ore is a crude material which requires working with, so a dream of this kind is alerting us that our opinions and ideas, though resourceful, can be somewhat crudely put and need refining. It may also be suggesting that we do not fully comprehend our own thoughts and we need to evaluate before speaking.

Organ

In traditional Chinese medicine, the various organs of the body depict different qualities. For example, the gall bladder handles our ability to make decisions, while the liver is the foundation of irritability. In dreams, therefore, being aware of a bodily organ would require us to be alert to what is bothering us and dealing with it in an appropriate way.

An organ in the sense of a musical instrument suggests grand sound and therefore one of high vibration.

Ornament

Ornaments, whether religious or secular, become part of our personal space, though the original intent was to enhance that space. In dreams it is this symbolism which is important. It may be, for instance, within a relationship that we feel undervalued and somewhat taken for granted, like an ornament. If so, we should act quickly to rectify the situation. On the other hand, it may be that we have something of meaning and worth that we wish to elevate to a better position. This of itself signifies that we need to use our own time and space more constructively in order to bring greater success.

Orphan

We all at some point in our lives feel deserted, unloved and vulnerable. It is not uncommon at this time to dream of an orphan. However, if we sense that we have been orphaned, then this might indicate that we need to stand on our own two feet and be more responsible. In another sense if we are taking care of an orphan, then it could be that we are trying to heal that part of us that feels uncared for.

Ouija Board

A Ouija board – an unrefined device used to contact the 'other side' – allows us to tap into the unknown which can sometimes become the dangerous unknown. So to dream of one suggests we need to explore the things we don't understand, to take risks and to confront our fears.

Outlaw

To dream of being an outlaw suggests we are aware of that part of us that feels it is beyond the laws of other men, both legally and morally. It has to do with that element (that most of us have) which aspires to be rebellious and anarchic. We must, however, endeavour to keep things in perspective.

Oval – *see* Shapes

Oven
When dreaming of an oven we are being made aware that we can transform some of our less developed traits into something more accessible and cultured. The old 'bun in the oven' saying does actually have some weight, as an oven can represent the womb as well as birth and gestation.

Owl
The owl is sacred to Athena, goddess of strategy and wisdom; therefore in a dream the owl can describe those qualities. Because it is also associated with the night-time, it can sometimes represent death.

Ox
The ox depicts the ability to be untiring, and to make sacrifices for others.

Oyster
Although there is no scientific evidence that the oyster encourages sexual desire, we should not dismiss the connected symbolism – all things sexual – that relates to it through dreams. The oyster also symbolises spiritual change. We can focus and build on negative qualities in our lives without trying to erase them completely.

Padlock

Dreaming of locking a padlock would mean that we are attempting to shut something – maybe an emotion – away. This links with another piece of symbolism, that is the need to defend ourselves from fear or possessiveness. Alternatively, if we are opening a padlock we may be trying to open up to new experiences.

Painting

Because painting has a lot to do with creative talent and self-expression, the way that we are painting in a dream may be important. If, for example, we are painting on a small canvas we may need to concentrate on detail. If we are painting large pictures we may need to adopt a wider perspective in our waking lives. Colour in a painting also has a bearing on interpretation.

Pairs

The unconscious mind has a knack of sorting information by comparing and contrasting. So when we are aware of conflict within ourselves, we may dream in pairs. In dream interpretation looking at the opposite meaning to the obvious can frequently give us a great deal of insight into our mental processes.

Pan

In dreams a pan signifies nurturing and caring. It can also suggest a receptive frame of mind. Just as a cauldron can be taken to indicate the transformative process, so a pan can suggest the ability to combine several 'ingredients' to make something completely different.

Paper

Paper is an image that, in dreams, is dependent on the circumstances in the dreamer's life. For example, in a student's life paper would suggest the need to pay attention to the studies. For a postman, there may be job anxieties, whereas festive wrapping paper could indicate the need for celebration. On a more universal level, paper can indicate a potential for learning and creativity.

Parachute
To dream of a parachute suggests that, whatever is happening to us in waking life, we have the protection that will see us through. It may also indicate that we are able to face our anxieties and still progress. A parachute can also denote freedom.

Paradise
To dream of Paradise is to link with the dreamer's inborn ability to be perfect. We can experience total harmony within ourselves. From another standpoint, paradise is that part of ourselves that is enclosed within, and does not need to be available to anyone else.

Paralysis
When paralysis is felt in a dream we are experiencing some kind of fear or suppression. Feelings that are emotionally based are felt as paralysis; this is to highlight the physical effect those feelings can have. The imagination can play tricks on us, and when we experience as real some kind of reaction we would not normally allow ourselves, it comes across as paralysis.

Parcel, Package – *see also* **Address**
If we receive a parcel, then we are being made aware of something we have experienced but not really explored. If we are sending a parcel, then we are releasing our energy. Both parcels and packages indicate potential and skill.

Parliament
If we dream of parliament, then we may need to make important decisions. Parliament also symbolises our recognition of a higher authority.

Party

When we dream we are attending a party, we are alerted to our social skills – or perhaps lack of them. In waking life we may be shy and dislike such gatherings, but in dreams, if we are coping with the groups and situations involved, we have a greater awareness of our own belonging. On a rather more obvious level, it may be that we need a celebration of some sort.

Passenger

In dreams, if we find that we are a passenger in a car the image most likely denotes that we are being carried along by circumstances, and have not planned for all eventualities. Travelling with one other passenger indicates that there may be a one-to-one relationship on the horizon, while carrying passengers suggests we may have knowingly or inadvertently made ourselves responsible for other people. This last image could suggest that other people are not pulling their weight in circumstances round us.

Passport

In waking life, a passport is used to prove identity; the passport appearing in a dream links with our own identity and self-image. It may also suggest, particularly if we have recently undertaken a new project, that we are allowing ourselves a passport to a better life.

Path

A path signifies the direction we have to take. This is pretty much all encompassing as it may represent the path of relationships, career, etc. We should try and identify if the path is smooth or rocky, winding or straight, as this will have a bearing.

Pattern – *see* Shape

Peacock

To see a peacock in a dream suggests an expansion of understanding from the plain and unadorned to the beauty of the fully plumed bird. Like the phoenix it represents rebirth and resurrection.

Pedestal

When we become conscious in a dream that something has been placed on a pedestal we have obviously attempted to make that thing special. We have elevated it to a position of power and worship – we have to decide if this is appropriate or not.

Pen/Pencil

If a pen or pencil appears in a dream we are expressing or recognising the need to communicate with other people. If the pen will not work we do not understand information we have been given. If we cannot find one we do not have enough information to proceed with an aspect of our lives. A pen suggests permanence; a pencil impermanence.

Pendant – *see* Necklace

Pepper

From a herb point of view, we probably need to liven up a situation to make it more interesting. In any case, pepper suggests that a radical change could be on the cards.

Perfume – *see also* Odour and Smell

It is likely that a certain perfume will remind us of a certain person or time – whether that is good or bad depends on the individual. Also, intuitive information is often recognised because of a particular perfume.

Pet

A pet appearing in a dream means we are linking in with our natural desire to give and receive love. We may need to 'look after' someone (or something), possibly more vulnerable than us. Pets represent unconditional love, affection and a mutual appreciation. A dead pet can represent the end of childhood or the loss of innocence.

Petrol

In dreams, petrol symbolises the energy we need to go places. Whether we are giving or receiving petrol will depend on whether we are reciprocating the energy.

Photographs

Photographs conjure up past occasions and memories – not all good, of course.

If we dream of looking at photographs we are often looking at some aspect of ourselves. To be given a photograph of oneself would indicate that we need to be taking an objective view of stuff around us or perhaps of ourselves within that situation – we need to stand back and look closely at what is going on.

Physician – *see* Doctor

Picture

A picture in a dream is usually an illustration of something that is part of our lives. It will depend on whether it is painted, or a print of another picture, as to the interpretation. The condition of the picture may be important, as may also the colours in the picture. The subject matter may give us suggestions as to what we should be 'looking at' in our lives.

Pig

The pig indicates foolishness, ignorance, selfishness, greed and dirtiness. The dreamer's better self may be beginning to recognise these unattractive qualities in himself. Without such recognition there can be no transformation or mastery of them. Big litters of piglets can represent fruitfulness, although sometimes without result, since the sow can depict the Destructive Mother.

Pier

A pier would suggest happy times and memories to most people. We may have an association with a particular town or it may simply be that a pier signifies rest and relaxation. It may also indicate the end of a journey.

Pilgrim/Pilgrimage

When we undertake a pilgrimage in a dream we recognise the purposeful, directed side of our personality. We have a goal in life, which may require a degree of faith to achieve. A pilgrim can often represent that part of our personality that is secure, and does not need external input; we have the ability to direct our lives provided we can create advantageous circumstances.

Pillar

One symbolism of a pillar relates to phallicism. Another, though, is probably more accurate. We are able to create stability and support and can stand firm in the presence of difficulty. In dreams, to find that we are a pillar of the community suggests that we should be taking more responsibility for our actions.

Pillow

Pillows, both in life and in dreams, indicate comfort and support. Sometimes, when we are going through a period of self-denial, we deny ourselves any comfort symbolism and so our pillow may disappear. To dream of a pillow fight indicates a mock conflict.

Pin

Here it depends whether the pin is holding something together or is being used to pierce us or some object in our dreams. If it is holding something together it indicates the emotional bonds we have. If it is piercing an object a trauma is suggested, although hopefully it will be quite small. Sometimes in dreams we are reminded of a feeling we have in everyday life. To experience the sensation of pins and needlessuggests that we are not ensuring an adequate flow of energy in a situation around us.

Pine Cone

If the pine cone does not have a personal connection for the dreamer – such as a childhood memory – it denotes good fortune. The shape of the pine cone and the fact that it contains many seeds gives an obvious connection to the phallus and masculinity.

Pipe

On a practical level a pipe symbolises many things. A water pipe can give information as to how we might handle our emotions. A tobacco pipe or chillum might suggest a means of escape, whereas a musical pipe indicates our connection with the rhythm of life.

Pistol – *see* **Gun**

Piston – *see also* **Engine**

A piston in a dream can mean sexual drive or activity. In this context it is more of a mechanical action than a loving act, and may show the dreamer's attitude to sex. A piston may also suggest a person's drive for success. The dreamer may need to assess the amount of effort that is necessary for him or her to be able to achieve their goals.

Pit – *see* **Abyss**

Placenta

The baby in the womb will use the placenta as a source of nourishment, so for us it will indicate that we are reliant on others, those we are connected to. In another meaning, one of the biggest traumas to be gone through is separation from our mother, and the placenta acts as a cushion in this process. Dreaming of a placenta indicates our need for such a cushion at times of separation.

Plague

Plagues are generally caused by an imbalance in natural ecology so if we dream of a plague it suggests that we have an imbalance from which we will suffer – whether it is physical, mental or emotional – within ourselves. The plague has obvious links with religion, so on that level it signifies Divine Retribution.

Plank – *see also* **Wood**

To dream of walking the plank suggests taking an emotional risk. A plank of wood appearing in a dream can indicate that something needs repairing, or that we feel safer carrying our own means of support. If the plank is to be used in flooring, the symbol is of security, but if to be used as a door or as decoration, it signifies an adornment of one's inner space.

Plants – *see also* **Weeds**

Due to the natural process of growth and decay that plants go through, they become a symbol for progressive change. Many plants have both healing and magical qualities. Equally, and as with all things, without proper knowledge plants can be harmful.

Play

When in a dream we are watching a play, we need to decide whether it is a drama, a comedy or a tragedy or if it's good or bad. This is because we often are trying to view our own lives objectively. More practically, it links with our creative side.

Plumage

Plumage being drawn to our attention can often stand for a display of our power and strength in achieving what we want. It may also be a signal of defiance, and we need to stand firm and show our colours.

Plumbing

Dreaming about plumbing is to look at the way we direct our emotions. It indicates how we make use of our emotions by avoiding obstacles and creating security for ourselves, thus controlling the flow of emotions within. Another interpretation is that of the internal plumbing. Often, to dream of plumbing in this sense alerts us that we should take care.

Plunge

To dream of plunging into something is to recognise that we are facing uncertainty. We are taking a risk and going into the unknown. That risk will often take us into our emotional depths and we will learn new things about ourselves which we will then be able to make use of. Also, to dream of plunging is to recognise that we have the ability to go forward.

Pocket

To dream of a pocket is to be dealing with one's personal secrets or thoughts – those things that we have deliberately chosen to hide rather than share. Following on from that, and on another level, a pocket can symbolise the Occult.

Point

Anything pointed refers to male sexuality. To be aware of the point of decision is to come to the conclusion that something has to be done – we must bring about change in one way or another and at that particular 'point'. In other words, until we decide to take action nothing will be happen.

Pointing

When we dream of someone pointing, normally we are having our attention drawn to a particular object, feeling or place. We need to take note of both who is pointing it out to us and equally what they are pointing at – after all, it may be an indication of the right direction for us. Alternatively, we may feel that we are at the receiving end – often pointing can be an aggressive act.

Poison

To be able to recognise poison in a dream means that we need to avoid an attitude, emotion or thought which will not be good for us. It indicates that there may be something about to contaminate us and therefore hold up our progress.

Pole

It will depend how the pole is being used in the dream as to its meaning. It is seen as an expression of the life force – as in a maypole – but also as a stabilising force or rallying point, as in a flagpole. It can also be a support mechanism.

Pool – *see also* Water

Dreaming of a pool deals with our need to understand our own emotions and inner feelings – we may need to submerge ourselves in our emotions to understand them. Other interpretations are: a pool in a wood suggests the ability to understand our own need for peace and tranquillity; an urban swimming pool may signify our need for structure in our relationships with other people whereas a pool in a road or path would suggest an emotional problem or difficulty needs to be dealt with before carrying out our plans.

Poppy

The poppy symbolises forgetfulness. In spiritual terms the soul must forget all it knows in order to reincarnate and rediscover its own awareness. The Great Mother as the Goddess was, and is, responsible for that forgetting – hence the poppy signifies the Great Mother.

Poverty
To encounter poverty in a dream highlights a sense of being deprived of the ability to satisfy our fundamental needs. If it is more to do with poor surroundings, then we have to look at things around us, rather than be introspective.

Prayer – *see also* **Religious Imagery**
Prayer denotes the idea that we need to help ourselves by seeking outside help. We may need someone else's authority to succeed in what we are doing. Psychologically, the human being has always needed to feel that there is a greater power than himself available to him.

Pregnancy
Dreaming of pregnancy suggests a fairly protracted waiting period necessary for something, possibly the completion of a project. Oddly, to dream of pregnancy seldom actually means one's own pregnancy, although it can indicate pregnancy for someone around us. Another meaning of dreaming about pregnancy centres around our being patient and waiting for a natural process to take place so that we can fulfil a particular task.

Present
When a present appears in a dream, it can be a play on words. We are being given a 'here and now' – we are being reminded to live in the moment, and not the past or future. If we are receiving a present we are being recognised as well as gaining from a relationship. If we are giving a present, we appreciate that we have characteristics we are able to offer other people. A pile of presents in a dream can signify as yet unrecognised talents and skills.

Pressure
When in waking life we are aware of pressure, this can be symbolised in

dreams as being pushed and can sometimes highlight our fear of illness. In certain forms of mental illness, the patient experiences a feeling of being pushed around and made to do something he does not want to do. Now and again, when experienced in dreams, this can actually be a form of healing.

Prison – *see also* **Key and Lock**

Prison, in dreams, denotes the traps we create for ourselves. We sometimes create a prison for ourselves through duty – for example, in relationships – or by guilt. And at this time, we can often see no way out.

Prize

In dreams to win a prize is to have succeeded in overcoming various obstacles.

In another meaning, gaining a prize in a dream means having used one's instincts and intuition in harmony in order to be able to use inspiration.

Propeller

A propeller acknowledges the drive and ambition behind our journey of progression and discovery. Recognising our needs, we also need to understand how to move forward. The action of a propeller is to give us 'lift', which suggests being able to use the intellect.

Public House

To be in a pub in a dream and aware of our behaviour indicates how we relate to groups and what our feelings are about society. A public space where we can drop inhibitions has links with our need for celebration. As a meeting place where generally few judgements are made, it becomes a place in which people can co-exist.

Pulling

If, in a dream, we are pulling, then this suggests a positive action. We are being alerted to the fact that we can do something about a situation. If we are being pulled we may feel that we are having to give in to outside pressure. In slang terms, pulling means picking up a potential partner. In dreams this can actually translate itself into a physical feeling. We may also, in everyday life, be being pulled in a certain direction – against our wishes – by our emotions and feel that we are powerless to resist.

Pulse

A pulse is the essential rhythm to life: without it we 'die'. To be aware in sleep of one's pulse may indicate some kind of anxiety. In dreams this may translate itself into a rhythm that is external to ourselves. There could also be health worries.

Punishment

When there is fear of retribution from an external source, we will often dream of being punished. Self-punishment occurs when we have not achieved the standards we expect of ourselves or if there is conflict in our lives. If we cannot resolve it we will often dream of being punished.

Puppet

When a puppet appears in a dream there is often a sense of being able to manipulate circumstances or people around us. If someone else is working the puppet, we may feel that it is we who are being manipulated. If the puppet is manipulating us, then we need to be aware of some sort of official difficulty. We may also sense that, as the puppet, we are part of something bigger.

Purse

In dreams a purse takes on a value of its own, because it holds what is valuable to us – usually money. The old saying, 'You cannot make a silk purse out of a sow's ear' has relevance in dreams as well as life. The mind can play tricks and manifest an apparently inappropriate image – one that needs to come under further inspection.

Pyramid

A pyramid is an extremely strong image. In dreams it exists on different levels; on a physical level, it is a building of wonder; on a mental level, it is a structure of regeneration: on a spiritual level, it is a guardian of power. It will depend on the level of awareness in the dreamer as to which interpretation it relates to.

Quarantine

Dreaming of having to put an animal into quarantine suggests our inability to look after a vulnerable part of ourselves, or others. When in normal life we feel isolated, this may translate itself in dream language as being in quarantine. It would seem that 'authority' has taken over to manage this isolation.

Quartz

Quartz seen in dreams tends to represent the crystallisation of ideas and feelings. It touches into our internal process, often enabling us to express that which we have found impossible before. Really, to dream of quartz signifies a recognition of developing power.

Quarry

To dream of a quarry is to be plumbing the depths of our personality, searching for any positive knowledge and intuition we may have hidden, in the hope of bringing it to a more conscious plane.

Queen

Such a figure, not only the present queen but a historical one, most often represents the dreamer's relationship with his mother, and thus with women in authority generally.

Quest

The Hero's Quest is an archetypal image that can appear in many guises in dreams. To be searching for something usually signifies that we are aware that we must undertake a frightening task in order to progress. Many fairy stories and mythological tales have as their main theme the search for something magical. Such themes can be translated into dreams on a personal level.

Question

To be asking questions in a dream indicates a degree of self-doubt. To have someone asking the dreamer questions shows us we are aware that we have some knowledge to share. If the question cannot be answered, the dreamer may need to seek the answer himself in waking life. If we have a question in waking life that needs answering, by keeping it in mind before going to sleep we may often find the answer through dreams.

Quicksand

Quicksand signifies a lack of security, possibly in all aspects of our life. To find ourselves trapped in quicksand suggests that we have been put in a difficult situation that is not necessarily of our own making.

Quilt

To dream of a quilt (or duvet) is, on all planes, to identify our need for security, warmth, care and love. A particular quilt may have a special significance. For instance, a childhood quilt in an adult dream would suggest the need for some kind of reassurance.

Quip

When we become aware of a joke or quip by someone else in a dream, we are recognising that we can allow ourselves to be affected by other people's sense of humour. If we are the ones who are communicating through wit or sarcasm, we may often be surprised by our own ability.

Quiver

Quivering symbolises extreme emotion. It may be an emotion that has surfaced because of a past experience and now needs addressing. On a more physical level, it could be that we are feeling the cold.

Quote/Quotation

To be giving a quote – as in a building estimate – can signify the value that we put on our talents. If we have difficulty with the accuracy – or the acceptance – of the quote we need to reconsider our own self-image. To hear a quote would suggest we should 'listen' to the sentiment being expressed. On another plane, a quotation signifies Truth.

R

Rabbit

Rabbits have obvious connections with fertility in dreams, or the trickster aspect of the personality could be coming to the fore (see Hare). A white rabbit may show the dreamer the way to the inner spiritual world and as such act as a guide.

Radiance

If something is distinguished by its radiance it has a special significance or quality that we should look at more closely, with pure thought and wisdom our main concerns.

Radio

Heading the symbolism here is communication. There may be information or ideas available to us that we need to listen to and understand more fully. The radio also signifies 'a voice of authority', so we should find that person whom we look up to and whose opinions we can take on board.

Raffle

To dream of a raffle – particularly of taking part in one – might suggest that we want to gain something in an easier fashion than by effort or hard work. A more charitable act than most forms of gambling, it may in drteams represent a quietening of our conscience at having taken a risk.

Railway

Dreaming of railways indicates that we have some tiny indecision on our mind. That is, we are wondering if, in life, we are on the right track and if not which way to go. If, in the dream, we can see only one track, then there may be only one way to go. If we can see more than one, then we have more opportunities and need to take a little more time choosing our way forward.

Rain

Appropriately, rain indicates tears and the releasing of pent up emotions. If we have been feeling low, then we are being made to realise that now is the time to let go. Rain as itself, as well as symbolically, can refresh and wash away. It may be that we need to clean ourselves of someone or something. It may also represent the sexual act.

Rainbow

To dream of a rainbow is normally a good thing as it is an indication of better things on the horizon. It can also mean that we have been hoping for, and now we are literally dreaming, of something better, something 'over the rainbow' as it were. From an esoteric standpoint, a rainbow is said to depict the seven steps of awareness necessary for true spirituality.

Ram

The ram is a symbol of masculine potency and authority, and, by association with those qualities, of the sign of Aries in the Zodiac.

Rat

The rat signifies the contaminated and devious part of the dreamer or of his situation. It can also represent something which is repellent in some way. Traditional symbolism suggests that the dreamer may be experiencing disloyalty from a friend or colleague.

Rape – *see* Sex

Raven

The raven, if it is seen to be talking, often represents prophecy. Its meaning can be ambivalent since it can represent evil and sin, but also wisdom.

Reading

Reading a book indicates that we are actively seeking knowledge or information. Also, to be aware that we are reading a novel is to begin to understand our own need for fantasy. A psychic reading often uses many basic dream images. To dream of having such a reading suggests a need to understand ourselves on a deeper level. Reading, or being in a library, appears in dreams as a form of spiritual realisation.

Reaping

In the song *Perfect Day*, Lou Reed sings "you're going to reap just what you sow", and to dream of reaping indicates just that: that there is a way to gain from work done. Also, if we dream of 'reaping a reward' for something we have done, we are approving of our own activities. On a more negative tack, a hurtful act could return to haunt us. Possibly even more negative is The Grim Reaper, often pictured with a scythe; he is said to reap in the dead.

Red – *see* Colours

Reflection

A reflection seen in a dream has a lot to do with the way we see ourselves or our self-image at that particular moment. It could also be a warning against self-worship. Also, we may be attempting to understand our inner working and the way in which we deal with everyday life.

Refrigerator

A symbol of self-preservation. On a practical level it could simply be that the bedroom is cold. You may have turned away on your side – that is, emotionally as well as sexually. This could be a result of stored up resentment, and therefore emotions will not grow.

Religious Imagery

We all hold within ourselves a personal basic truth. Religious imagery, because it is so universal, helps us to link back to that basic 'truth'. Despite cultural differences there are certain aspects of this imagery which are universally recognised. An icon –a statue or a painting – though more often thought of within orthodox religion, is actually an illustration of a religious concept. For instance, the statue of the Virgin Mary in Christianity has the same inherent meaning as Durga, the goddess of devotion in Hinduism.

When such symbolism begins to appear in dreams it is time for the dreamer to begin to access the inner truth or spirituality which we all possess, and to take responsibility for his or her life. Depending on the culture and/or knowledge the images will often be startlingly specific in their symbolism. Christian images will tend to appear more readily for people within a society whose law is based on the Ten Commandments. Other systems of belief will manifest their own images.

In the following section an attempt has been made to include the types of dream images which most often appear:

Angels It is important to distinguish between the 'higher self' and the angelic form. Angels tend to be androgynous and to represent pure being and freedom from sin. When the image of a 'dark' angel appears in dreams it usually suggests that we are being alerted to some kind of spiritual wrong doing that has probably already taken place. Angels are seen as messengers from the gods.

Baptism This is a rite of initiation into the family of man, and in dreams suggests a ceremony or ritual of welcome, marking a particular stage of development.

Bible/religious texts If we dream of a Bible or other religious book, it usually means that we are aware of traditional moral standards. We need a code of conduct which helps us to survive and there is such a resource available to us.

Buddha The figure of Buddha in dreams highlights our ability to experience life to its fullest extent, and those qualities of 'being' which are necessary to be able to do this.

Ceremony Ceremony and ritual form an integral part of religion and also mark the various rites of passage which are necessary as we grow towards maturity. In dreams, taking part in such ceremonies usually denotes a change in attitude, belief or awareness.

Christ Christ personifies 'perfect man' demonstrating the reconciliation of the spiritual and the physical – God and man. Seen in his various aspects, such as appearing on the cross, he represents that part of us which is prepared to suffer for our beliefs.

Churches, chapels synagogues, temples etc. Religious buildings usually suggests sanctuary, feelings of awe or a place where we can share our beliefs.

Crucifixion Often represents sacrifice made in the name of principle.

Demon/Devil Seen as temptation, such figures can signify suppressed sexual drives and desires. For most, such figures are the personification of evil.

Feathered Sun This symbol appears in a number of cross cultural religious images, drawing together the symbols of the Sun and the Eagle. It indicates the universe and the centre of ourselves – the universal centre and solar power.

Festivals In waking life festivals were developed by religious leaders as an opportunity for people to meet together for celebration and sharing. They continue to have this meaning in dreams, as well as pinpointing the various times of year at which the festivals take place. Pagan festivals such as Beaten were adopted by conventional religions in order to give continuity to worship rituals.

God/Gods When we dream of God we are acknowledging to ourselves that there is a higher power more knowing and able than we are. Throughout one stage of development there is comfort and security in believing that there is a paternal God who will care for us and approve of us, and the forceful emotions we sometimes encounter may be linked with our childhood need for love and parental approval. In a woman's dream, dreaming of mythical gods will help her to understand various aspects of her own personality. In a man's dream he is linking with his own masculinity and his sense of belonging to himself, and therefore to the rest of humanity.

Christian belief holds to one God, although manifesting in three forms – Father, Son and Holy Ghost. (Jehovah, in the sense of a vengeful god, alerts us to the negative side of power.) Other religions attribute the powers to various Gods. As we grow in understanding, we can appreciate the relevance of both beliefs and can begin to understand God as an all pervading energy.

Goddess/Goddesses Dreaming of goddesses connects us with our archetypal images of femininity. In a woman's dream a goddess will clarify the connection through the unconscious that exists between all women and female creatures. It is the sense of mystery, of a shared secret, which is such an intangible force within the woman's psyche. In the waking state it is that which enables women to create. To dream about goddesses, therefore, is to accept our right to initiation into a sisterhood or network in order to bring about a common aim. In a man's dream the goddess figure signifies all that a man fears in the concept of female power. It usually also gives an insight into his earliest view of femininity through his experience of his mother.

Through her understanding of the goddesses, a woman will come to terms with her own essential nature.

Hell The old fashioned image of hell suggests a state of illusion, where nothing is ever as it seems. In dreams, to be aware of hell suggests that the dreamer is beginning to understand his or her chaotic nature.

Heaven In dreams, heaven is represented as a place of high energy, where there is no suffering. Such an idea is seen in most religions, and more often than not manifests when the individual is becoming more spiritually orientated.

Holy Communion/Manna/Spiritual Food Any image in dreams of sharing food, particularly bread, in a religious setting, has the symbolism of holy communion, a sacred sharing of the power that belongs to God. This has its roots in the pagan belief that all power and energy can be shared.

Holy Mother These images in dreams such as that of the Virgin Mary signify the whole essence of feminine nurturing and holiness associated with the figure of the mother.

The Holy Man or Woman The holy man or woman appearing in dreams signifies the inner guidance, which is available to all.

Incense This symbolises a request and a prayer offered to God or to the gods, through perfume and smoke. For those who have knowledge the perfume used may be important.

Pope Often, to meet the Pope in a dream is to meet the side of ourselves which has developed a code of behaviour based on our religious beliefs. He may be benign or judgmental depending on how the figure of the Pope was presented in childhood. The Pope often appears in dreams as a substitute for the father, or as a personification of God.

Priest or prophet The appearance of such a figure indicates an inner awareness of a belief system, sometimes in the future.

Religious Service or Ritual

In dreams, rituals or ceremonies highlight the idea of certain of the actions having meaning whether individually or in sequence. Indeed, it is often the cumulative effect of the actions which is seen to be important. It is also necessary to understand the effect of group behaviour in such services.

Rent
Whenever we undertake a personal responsibility in waking life, it is often symbolised by dreaming of paying rent in some way. Receiving rent, on the other hand, indicates that we have entered into a negotiation that will benefit us in the long run, that we have understood material value. It is also a symbol of security.

Reptiles
Reptiles in dreams connect with our basic and instinctive reactions and responses. When there is a need to understand why we do things we first need to control, understand and manage our basic drives.

Rescue
When we are rescued in a dream we are aware that we are then indebted to our rescuer. The knight rescuing the maiden symbolises the notion of the untouched feminine being rescued from her own passion. On another level it could be that we need rescuing from ourselves.

Resign
In dreams, to resign signifies, literally, to give up. We need to know if this a good or bad thing. It could be that we cannot face the music that life presents to us. If this is the case we need to assure ourselves that no further effort can be put in. It may be that we need to try harder.

Ribbon - *see* Bridle

Right
The right side signifies the more controlling, logical and confident side, which perceives the outside world in a impersonal fashion. It is to do with 'rightness', that is propriety, morality and social behaviour. Anything observes on the right-side in dreams is usually significant as the

dreamer progresses. Any pain experienced on the right-side can also be interpreted in terms of motivation. It also expresses the more masculine attributes. Movement to the right indicates that something is coming into conscious awareness. The conflict between right and left is usually between logic and intuition.

Ring

A ring is continuous and self-perpetuating, so, appearing in a dream, normally suggests a relationship. Because of this there are different meanings for different rings. A signet ring would imply setting the seal on something. A wedding ring symbolises commitment. A 'family' ring represents tradition and value. An engagement ring hints at a tentative promise of devotion. An eternity ring would be a long term promise.

Rivers or streams – *see also* Water

Like roads, these denote the dreamer's life and the way that he or she is living it at that moment. It will depend on the dreamer's attitude or state of mind as to whether he sees his life as a large river or a small stream. If the water in the river appears to be contaminated we are not deciding on the best actions for ourselves, and may be letting others affect our judgement. Crossing a river means there will be great changes, but can sometimes suggest death, either of the self or of the old. If the river is very deep we should perhaps be paying attention to how we relate to the rest of the world, and our feelings about it. If the river is rushing by we may feel that life is moving along at too fast a pace. If we can see the sea as well as the river, we may be aware that a great change must occur, perhaps an expansion of consciousness, or that greater attention must be paid to the unconscious within. If the river causes us to be frightened we are creating an unnecessary difficulty for ourselves by not understanding our emotions.

Road

Just as individual vehicles demonstrate a dreamer's body and external way of being, so the road reflects the dreamer's way of doing things. For instance, a road which meanders all over the place may indicate that we have no real sense of direction. Any turns in the road, particularly a blind corner, will suggest changes of direction; cross-roads will offer choices, while a cul-de-sac would signify a dead end. Any obstacle in the road will reflect difficulties on the chosen path, and if a particular stretch of road is accentuated it may be a period of time, or may mean an effort. Going up hill will suggest extra effort, while going down hill will suggest lack of control.

Robe

If we dream of, say, a bath robe this indicates two things. One is the covering up of nakedness, the other is a sense of being at ease. To be dressing someone else is to be protecting them. A robe can symbolise our thoughts, relationships and sex, with clean and dirty being the operative words. In the magical sense, a robe can suggest status and power; the white robe symbolises innocence, while the seamless robe represents holiness.

Rock

To dream of rock might indicate that we need a more solid foundation in the real world. On another tack, seaside rock – that is edible – can remind us of happier more carefree times. This image may represent the need to recognise various qualities within ourselves that are connected with rock, such as reliability, coldness, rigidity, and then deal with them appropriately. Dual rocks through which we must pass suggest the same image as the passage between two pillars, that is, passing from one state of being to the next.

Rocket

On a base level the rocket is connected with male energy and sexuality. A rocket is also a symbol of power, so we may need to look at whether or not we can do things better then we previously thought. A rocket can also represent a search for something more spiritual and 'out of this world' in our lives.

Rocking

Rocking in dreams can be a comforting activity, like a child who will rock himself to sleep. Rocking can also suggest infantile behaviour, from the point of view that it puts us in touch with the natural rhythms of life. This gentle movement also helps us touch in with our own centre, but is also a symbol of transition.

Roof

To dream of being under a roof allows us to acknowledge the shelter and protection it gives. Obviously if the roof is leaking or we are on the roof, then we are leaving ourselves open to emotional attack. The sheltering aspect of the feminine as the guardian of the hearth is sometimes represented as a roof.

Rooms

While the function of each room is important, rooms can have significance in dreams in other ways. A small room with only one door or a basement with water in it is a very direct representation of the womb, and may suggest a need to return to the womb-like state, or a consideration of issues to do with pregnancy. A series of rooms refers to the various aspects of femininity, and often to the whole soul. Something in an upstairs room denotes an idea or concept belonging to the spiritual or intellectual realms. Leaving a room and going into another one suggests leaving something behind in order to bring about change. Such a change need not necessarily be for the better. If a room is empty something, such as comfort or support, is lacking in our lives.

Root – *see* Tree

Rope

A rope can indicate strength and power. The power, however, can turn against us. If the rope is made of an unusual material there is some special bond or necessity that requires the qualities of that essence. If we are tied to the rope, something is holding us back from expressing ourselves. Being tied by a rope to something else means we need to look at the relationship between us and what we are tied to.

Rose

The rose in dreams, as in life, often represents love, admiration and perfection. Dreaming of a rose can also suggest fertility and virginity. Through its own cycle of growth and decay the rose can symbolise the cycle of life. It also represents the heart centre of life.

Round Table
A round table, like the symbolism of a ring, suggests wholeness – but more essentially the idea that everyone is equal. The table also indicates a centre, but one from which all things can begin.

Ruins
When something is left in ruins we have to ascertain if it is through carelessness or vandalism. If the former, the suggestion is that we need to get things together. If the latter, we need to look at how we are allowing ourselves to be vulnerable.

If we have deliberately ruined something we need to acknowledge the self-destructive element in us.

Running
When running occurs in a dream we need to establish the time and place as this will have a bearing on the symbolism. As an example, one of the most common 'running' dreams is that of actually not being able to run away from somebody; this indicates fear and an inability to do something – a common element in anxiety dreams.

Rust
Rust symbolises neglect and lethargy, both emotionally and physically. To dream of rust means we have to clean up our act before we can progress. If we don't, we will suffer. Rust can also signify outdated attitudes.

S

Saddle

A saddle appearing in a dream will indicate a need to exercise control over someone. For a woman this is often sexual control; for a man it is more likely that his own life needs management.

Sadism – *see also* **Sex**

Sadism often surfaces because of anger held over – but suppressed – from childhood pain. It is the wish to hurt or provoke a reaction – often in someone we love. In the dream we have to recognise if we are being sadistic or having a form of sadism inflicted upon us. Both can represent parts of ourselves.

Sailing – *see also* **Boats**

Sailing suggests a sense of freedom and the chance to use our intellect. It can also bring into focus the way we are directing our lives. If we are sailing in a yacht there is more of a sense of immediacy than if we were sailing, say, in a liner. The first is more to do with one-to-one relationships, while the second suggests more of a group effort.

Sailor

A sailor represents freedom of movement and spirit as he is in total control of his own destiny. For a woman, the sailor as with other uniformed figures, can appear as the Hero, he is a romanticised representation of the heroic figure. For a man this image is more to do with being given permission to run free.

Salt

In dreams, the image of salt highlights the refined qualities we bring to our lives, those things we do to enhance our lifestyle. For the most part, we run our lives through our emotions but the more subtle aspects are just as vital. As a symbol of permanence and incorruptibility salt is also important in dreams.

Sand
Sand in a dream suggests instability and a lack of emotional security. Sand can also represent impermanence. It may be that the foundations we are working from do not have a solid enough base, and are likely to 'shift' at any moment.

Sap
In dream terms sap indicates that we are now ready to undertake new work or perhaps even a new relationship. We are aware of our own strength and vitality and are prepared to take on a new challenge. In another way a 'sap' is a more affectionate term for 'wimp'. It may be that we need to get a bit of backbone into our lives.

Satellite
A satellite signifies communication. It suggests an efficient, effective way of contact and relation. A satellite can also appear in a dream to alert us to a dependency that one person can have upon another – though this need not be a bad thing.

Savings – *see* Money

Saw – *see* Tools

Scaffold
A scaffold in a dream will normally indicate that there is some kind of temporary structure in our lives. If it is a hangman's scaffold this will suggest that a part of our lives must come to an end. Either way, a scaffold denotes that some change needs to occur in our lives.

Scales
Scales (astrologically represented by the sign of Libra) in a dream suggest the need for balance and self-control in our world. The type of scale we see in our dream will determine the meaning. Bathroom scales would

suggest a more personal assessment is required, whereas a weigh bridge might suggest that we need to take our whole lives into consideration. If they were doctor's scales we may be alerting ourselves to a potential health problem.

Scalp – *see* **Head** *under* **Body**

Scar
A scar in a dream tells us that there are old wounds that have not been fully dealt with. These may be emotional as much as physical. It is often important which part of the body is scarred, as our nervous system has ways of giving information through our dreams.

School
In situations where we are learning new abilities or skills, the image of a school, or 'school of life' will often appear in dreams. However, we may also be learning about the nature of people and relationships. Alternatively, a school will often appear at a time when we are attempting to get rid of antiquated ideas and concepts.

Scissors
In dreams scissors denote cutting the non essential out of our lives. These may be things that we simply cannot deal with, and it is now time to cut them out. On a more 'out there' level, scissors have ambivalent significance. They can cut the Thread of Life, but can also represent unity and the coming together of the spiritual and physical.

Screw
It rests on what culture we belong to as to how we are going to interpret a screw. In the criminal circle a screw will mean a prison officer or jailer and therefore authority in general. To the younger element in society it is used, along with a number of others words, as slang for the sexual act. So we need to look out for word play, even if the object seen is a proper screw. Screws can also suggest a task that, in itself, we may consider pointless on its own, but which becomes more significant in a wider context.

Scroll

If we dream of a scroll we are endorsing the knowledge or information that has been given to us, so that we can now enhance our lives. A scroll can also represent hidden knowledge as well as the passing of time.

Scythe – *see also* Sickle

The scythe is a cutting instrument, and has a similar symbolism to that of a knife. Its appearance will alert us to some very deeply held notions and ideas. The scythe, as used by the Grim Reaper, also represents death.

Sea or Ocean

The original chaotic state from which all life emerges is often pictured as a sea. It usually depicts cosmic consciousness, that is a state of total knowledge, although that may be obscured by our fear of 'the deep'. We need not fear that which we understand. A shallow sea suggests insincere emotion. The waves in the sea characterise emotion and lust. A calm sea suggests a peaceful existence, while a stormy sea signifies passion, either negative or positive. To be conscious of the rise and fall of the tides is to be conscious both of the passage of time and of the rise and fall of our own emotions.

Seal

A seal can represent hidden knowledge, authority and power. In dreams, the ownership of a seal gives us the authority to take responsibility for our own actions. If we are seen to be breaking a seal, then this might indicate we are betraying a confidence.

Searchlight

If a searchlight appears in a dream, then we need to focus our attention and concentrate more fully on matters that concern us. A searchlight is used to show the way ahead, as is a torch.

Seasons

When we are made aware of the seasons of the year in dreams, we are also connecting with the various periods of our lives. Spring signifies childhood; Summer, young adulthood; Autumn, middle age; Winter, old age. It could also be alerting us to the need for enjoyment, as the seasons are also connected with celebration and festival.

Seed

A seed symbolises our potential. For a woman, though, it may also suggest pregnancy. A seed can also indicate the validity of something we are planning. We need to have the right conditions in which to grow and mature.

Serpent – *see also* **Snake**

The serpent is a universal symbol which can be male or female or it can be self-created. It can signify death or destruction or conversely life and also rejuvenation. It is the instinctive nature and is also potential energy. When the power of the instinctive nature is understood and harnessed the dreamer comes to terms with his or her own sexuality and sensuality, and is able to make use of the higher and more spiritual energies which become available. **In a man's dream** a serpent may appear if he has not understood the feminine or intuitive part of himself, or when he doubts his own masculinity. **In a woman's dream** the serpent may manifest if she is afraid of sex, or sometimes of her own ability to seduce others. Because of its connection with the Garden of Eden the serpent is the symbol of duplicity and trickery, and also of temptation.

Sex

A child's first appreciation of itself is as a separate entity from its mother and has to cope with the separation from her. It becomes aware of its need to be protected, comforted and loved.

A crucial stage of its development is its fascination with its own body, and what feels comfortable and good, whether it is nice to touch or be touched, or indeed if touch is permissible. A fear of being touched may reveal itself in dreams, and be recognised as a sexual problem even though the original trauma may have been kept hidden. It is when the individual is no longer afraid of the curiosity that allows an innocent exploration of his own body, that real growth can begin. Dreams will often allow us to explore this physicality in a safe and very personal way.

The complete range of the individual's sexuality can be revealed in dreams. If we ignore our own sexual nature and fail to acknowledge our life force, then the negative aspects will make themselves known in dreams – this is nature's attempt at levelling out the waking state where this awareness may be over intellectualised or over dramatised. Interaction with others then becomes essential, and this need will often make itself apparent in dreams.

There are many aspects of sex and sexuality to be interpreted and explained, beginning here with **bisexuality**. As individuals we carry both masculine and feminine potential and responses. One is often more obvious than the other, and there can additionally in some cases be conflict between the internal and external. This sometimes shows itself in dreams as bisexuality or a need for a bond with members of both sexes.

Dreaming of **castration** indicates a fear of losing our masculinity or even our sexual prowess – a common fear amongst men.

To dream of **clothing** in a sexual context can have specific relevance to the dreamer's perception of him or herself. For example, dreaming of being fully clothed during sex would signify some degree of guilt, either on the part of the dreamer or of someone close to them.

Contraception can indicate a fear of pregnancy or of responsibility, for both men and women. More specifically for women there might be a fear of giving birth.

In dreams, **fetishes** – fixations on an external object without which there can be no sexual act – can highlight fear, immaturity and lack of capability. There is evidence substantiating the belief that, at an unconscious level, man would go for a life of celibacy and that by focusing his energies onto an object he relinquishes responsibility for the sexual act.

Dreaming of a **hermaphrodite** (who has both masculine and feminine sexual organs) can indicate either bisexuality, or androgyny – the ideal balance within one person of masculine and feminine qualities.

Universally, **homosexuality** is understood as the desire for sex with a partner who is the same sex. However, a more correct definition is the desire for someone who is the same or very similar to oneself. It is this element that comes across in dreams. If, on reflection, the dreamer can identify similarities in ways which are not purely sexual the dream can be interpreted more fully.

Images appearing in a dream preceding orgasm can signify the real nature of the dreamer's attitude to sex and sexuality. The conflicts and problems which arise in the dreamer because of his sexual desire for someone can be dealt with in the dream state through dreaming of emission or orgasm.

Incest in a dream usually symbolises the desire to express love or have it expressed in a warmer, more tactile way. More obviously, dreaming of incest can highlight guilty feelings about one's parents or members of the family.

The need to be able to communicate properly with someone, on a more intimate level, can show itself as **intercourse** in a dream. If intercourse is interrupted the dreamer may have inhibitions of which he or she is not consciously aware. Also, intercourse in a dream can denote the integration of a particular part of one's personality – if a child is then born that integration has been or can be considered a success.

A **kiss** can indicate a mark of respect, or a desire to stimulate the dream partner. It indicates we should be aware of what arousal we need for ourselves.

The desire to hurt oneself or to be hurt through sex in dreams highlights **masochism**. This often arises from two causes. The first is to play the martyr – to suffer for one's sins. The second is to feel exceptional emotion of one sort or another. It may be we are not allowing ourselves to feel deeply in everyday life.

Dreaming of **masturbation** is to do with the need for comfort and, for a younger person, the excitement and innocence of exploration.

When some kind of image that we as the dreamer consider to be sexually **perverted** appears, we are avoiding or attempting to avoid issues to do with closeness and bonding.

If ideas of **rape** appear in a dream, then it can be as much to do with violation of personal space as with the sexual act. Sexual rape is unlikely to appear in the dreams of sexually abused children, though the adult may later suffer from nightmares. Rape itself may only manifest when the adult is ready to deal with the trauma. Most rape dreams are based around the need for, or perception of, power issues between the male and female.

Sadism appearing in a dream highlights a counter balance to the dreamer's conscious way of being in the world. In everyday life the dreamer may be either very placid, in which case it is an escape valve; or if the dreamer has to be dominant and controlling in everyday life the unconscious is showing its need for freedom.

Dreams have a crazy way of throwing up pictures of primitive rites and practises of which we may have no conscious knowledge. **Semen** is the sign of masculinity and physical maturity and is often seen in dreams as other milky fluids. The spilling of such fluid can represent the sexual act as primeval.

Feeling desire for someone else, most often of the opposite sex, is a basic urge for closeness with that person. It seems that we are looking for a part of ourselves that we have lost and the other character represents the closest that we can get to it. If we were fully integrated we would have no need for sex with someone else, but for most of us there is a desire to be united with everything which is not part of our own ego. Such a dream, which highlights the feelings we are capable of having, provides a basis that enables us to understand our own needs Transvestism in dreams signifies a confusion so far as gender is concerned.

A dream where we are conscious of **venereal disease** suggests an awareness of some kind of infection. This need not always be of a sexual nature; it may also be emotional.

Sexual activity is either the highest expression of love and spirituality between two people, or if purely physical is entirely selfish. It would be up to the dreamer to determine which it is.

Shampoo
It may be that we need to clear our minds and our heads in order to see and think clearly. This is often symbolised in a dream by shampoo. In another, more lyrical way, it could be we need to wash someone out of our hair, so to speak.

Shapes
If and when geometric shapes appear in a dream, then we are given a greater understanding of the abstract world – depending on what stage of development we have reached at that point. It is as though the ancient perception of form is beginning to take on a new meaning and

signification. It is important to note as much as possible in the dream, as the number of sides the shape has will be significant, as will the colours. Generally, though, the dreamer can accept the nature of things as they are, and can take time to look at the basic structure of his own nature. He can appreciate the shape his life is taking without placing emotional inhibitions in the way.

The various shapes and patterns likely to be thrown up in dreams are interpreted thus; beginning with the **centre** – the point from which everything starts. In regard to shape, it is the point from which the pattern grows.

The **circle** symbolises the inner being or the Self. It is also totality and perfection. A circular object – such as a ring – may have the same meaning as the circle. A circle with a dot in the centre can signify the soul in completion. It is also sometimes taken to represent femininity.

The **crescent** also signifies the feminine, that is, the mysterious power that is intuitive and typically non rational.

Any **cross** appearing in a dream stands for the realisation (in the sense of making real) and moving of spirit into substance. Travelling through the symbol of the sword to the equal armed cross, from there to the cross of suffering and crucifixion, and finally to the Tau of perfection, the soul learns through experience to conquer the barricades, thus enabling spiritual progression. The hung cross with the figure of Christ symbolises the sacrifice of self for others. The four arms pointing in opposing directions signify conflicts, sorrow and torment, but these are ultimately necessary in order to reach perfection. The three upper arms are said to stand for God the Father, Son and Holy Ghost, though more clearly any Divine Trinity. The intersection signifies the reconciliation of opposites.

A **diamond** suggests that we have greater but fewer options available.

A **hexagram** symbolises the harmonious development of the physical, social and spiritual elements of human life and its cohesion in creating a perfect whole.

Symbolic of the womb is the **oval** shape, which also suggests feminine life. Called the Vesica Piscis, it is the halo that totally encircles a sacred figure.

In dreams, **patterns** such as mosaic or kaleidoscope, which appear as part of the dream scenario, can classify how we handle the patterns, and perhaps behavioural repetition, in our lives.

The **sphere** has a similar meaning to the globe, and denotes perfection and completion of all possibilities.

The **spiral**, meanwhile, is the ideal path to evolution and growth. The doctrine states that everything is continually in motion, but also continually rising or raising its vibration. If the spiral is towards the centre we advance towards our own centre by a roundabout route. A clockwise spiral, moving outward to the right is a movement towards consciousness and enlightenment. If counter clockwise, the movement is towards the unconscious, probably regressive behaviour. There is also a link with the navel or solar plexus, as the centre of power and energy.

The **square** or cube symbolises the manifestation of the spirit into the physical. It represents the earthly realm as opposed to the heavens. A square within a circle suggests the act of 'becoming' or taking on form. The figure within a square is the Self or perfect Man. Any square object signifies the enclosing and feminine principle.

The **star**, especially if it is a bright one, denotes those things we all reach for – hope, aspiration, and ideal. The five pointed star or pentagram evokes personal magic, and all matter in harmony. To be accurate, the star should point upwards. In dreams it symbolises the dreamer's ownership of his own magical qualities and wishes. If it is pointing downwards it symbolises the antithesis – evil and witchcraft. Twelve stars signify both the Twelve Tribes of Israel and the Apostles. The six pointed star, or Star of David, is made up of one triangle pointing upward and another pointing downward. Here, the physical and the spiritual are united in harmony creating wisdom.

The **swastika**, with its arms moving clockwise, portrays Ideal man and the power he has for good. In eastern symbolism it signifies the movement of the sun. Moving counter clockwise the swastika in this form signifies all that is sinister and wrong. In this respect it is not known whether Hitler – who had aspirations towards magic – deliberately chose this reversed swastika.

The **triangle** portrays standing man, with his three parts or being – body, mind and spirit. It also symbolises consciousness and love revealed through his physicality. If the triangle points upwards, human nature moves towards the divine. If it is pointing down it is spirit seeking expression through the physical. The triangle can also represent family relationships – that is, father, mother and child.

There is a game based on shapes in which you draw a square, a circle and a triangle, and then get someone else to elaborate each of the basic shapes into a drawing. Whatever he makes of the square is supposed to relate to his outlook on the world, the circle to his inner being, and the triangle to his sex life.

Shave

If it is a man dreaming of shaving, (it is likely he'll be shaving his face) this suggests that he is trying to change his image. If it is a woman, she is likely to be shaving other parts of her body in order to create a more beautiful image. Both indicate removing an unwanted layer, that is, a facade that has been created.

On another tack, if we sense that we have had a 'close shave' then it is possible that we are taking too many risks.

Sheep

The sheep is renowned for its flock instinct, and it is this interpretation which is most usually accepted in dreams. The helplessness of the sheep when off-balance is also another aspect which is recognisable, as is the apparent lack of intelligence. The god-fearing 'good sheep' and also the passive and 'sheepish' may have relevance within the context of the dream. to dream of sheep and wolves, or of sheep and goats is to register the conflict between good and evil.

Shells

A shell, in life as in dreams, is a form of defence that we use to prevent ourselves from being hurt emotionally. A shell can also be seen as a magical symbol that holds within it the power of transformation. Dreaming of a shell can also indicate that there is wisdom within us – a 'pearl' of wisdom.

Shelter

Shelter of any kind signifies protection. If we are giving shelter to someone in dreams, we may be protecting a part of ourselves from hurt or difficulty. If we are being given shelter we are conscious of the fact that there is protective power in our lives.

Shield
A shield is a symbol of preservation and growth. In our development as human beings, the shield may appear as a symbol of a particular stage of growth. It is at this point that the individual needs to acknowledge that he has control over his own destiny. Often this symbol first appears in dreams representing this stage of development.

Shop
In dreams, a shop signifies something that we feel we want or need. If it is a shop we know then we are most likely, aware of what we want from life. If it is an unknown shop, then we may have to search our minds for what we want. If we are out on a shopping spree, then we need to satisfy our desires and are willing to pay large amounts for it.

Shot, Shooting – *see also* Gun
When we are shot in a dream this indicates that our feelings have been hurt recently – or we have found ourselves a target for others' rage. If the dreamer is shooting something, he may be having to deal with his own fears. He could be guarding against meeting parts of his personality he does not like.

Shovel/Spade
A shovel in a dream will signal a desire to dig into past experiences for information – possibly from an introspective point of view. A garden spade would suggest a degree of pragmatism, whereas a fire shovel would symbolise a need to take care.

Shrinking
Firstly, on a psychological level we can learn to handle who we are by recognising both how necessary, and also how small, we are in the bigger picture. The latter can be accompanied by a feeling of shrinking. Therefore we become less threatening to ourselves and others. This links with a possible need to return to childhood.

Shroud

A shroud is linked with death, and can signify that we do not fully understand the subject. The image can be frightening, but if we are aware that by shrouding we are hiding something, then it becomes less so. It can also be taken as a mark of respect.

Sickness – *see also* Illness

To feel, or to be, sick, usually signals that there is something we need to get rid of; we may be 'sick`' of something or somebody When something is not right in our world, on any level, we need to abolish it. Sickness is one way of doing this.

Sickle

Now that we have moved from an agricultural to a more technological way of thinking, the sickle is no longer such an important image. What we are left with is the old symbol of the sickle representing mortality and death. As so often happens, this is not necessarily a physical death, but the death of part of ourselves.

Sieve

In dreams a sieve indicates our ability to make the right decision, the ability to sort the good from the bad. It can suggest that we have the knowledge available to know how to get the best out of ourselves.

Signature

Our signature in a dream signifies that we have an appreciation and a recognition of ourselves and our mark in the world. If our signature appears to be illegible, then this might suggest that we are not sure if we are going about things in the right way.

Silver

On one level silver can represent money or financial affairs – or certainly something we consider to be of value. On a totally different level silver symbolises the qualities of the moon. It could be that we want to reach for something or someone but we may now need to consider it only a remote possibility.

Singing

Singing is to do with self-expression. If we are singing, then we are expressing happiness. We may also be aware of our skill in expression.

If we are chanting, then this suggests that the dreamer is in touch with a higher vibration.

Sinking

To be sinking in a dream suggests we have lost confidence and are feeling afraid or hampered by a situation. Someone else sinking suggests we are aware of a difficulty that perhaps needs our assistance. What we are sinking into is often relevant. To be sinking in water would suggest a particular emotion is threatening to drown us. To be sinking in sand indicates that we feel there is no safe ground for us.

Siren

When we hear a siren in a dream, then we are being warned of forthcoming danger. A Siren, in the sense of an alluring woman, indicates deception and distraction of man from his direction. For a woman, the siren can be a destructive thing if not acknowledged.

Size

To be conscious of size in a dream highlights how we feel in relation to a person or object, remembering that in dreams size is relative. Big might suggest important or threatening, whereas small might indicate vulnerability and a degree of insignificance.

Skeleton

A skeleton indicates the 'bare bones' of something – an idea or concept – and also our own feelings about death. We are aware that the physical must 'die', but there is a framework – a reminder – left. A skeleton in a closet represents a past action or shame we wish to hide.

Skin – *see* Body

Skull

There is varied skull symbolism in dreams: to be aware of one's own skull is to recognise the structure that we have given our lives. To perceive a skull where there should be a head suggests that part of the person has 'died'. To be talking to a skull is recognising the need to communicate with people we have not heard from in a while. When a skull is talking to us, a part of us that we have rejected is coming back to life. If we believe in life after death, we may feel that the spirit is talking through the skull.

Sky

In dreams the sky can represent the mind. It can also signify our potential. If the sky is dark it may reflect our mood of gloominess; if it is bright, our mood of joy.

Smell – *see also* Odour *and* Perfume

To be aware of a smell in a dream usually reminds us of a time and a place that holds certain memories. Whether the smell is good or bad indicates the nature of its association.

Smoke/Smoking – *see also* Fire

Smoke in dreams suggests danger around the corner, especially if we cannot locate the fire. If we are smoking, we are attempting to control anxiety. If we smoke in real life, but recognise in dreams that we no longer do so, we have overcome a difficulty. Smoke, on another level, can signify prayer rising to heaven.

Snake – *see also* Serpent

Snake and serpent dreams occur usually when there is an aspect of sexuality or emotional passion that has not been understood and the dreamer must come to terms with his or her more instinctive self. Usually this part of the personality has been suppressed and thwarted and since the most primitive urge is sexuality, the image of the snake or serpent as sustained power is the most effective available. On a more basic level this has direct connotations with the penis.

The serpent is always taken to signify evil, as in the Garden of Eden, yet it actually represents uncontrolled passion. The serpent suggests temptation, yet also signifies the search for the spiritual. A snake entwined around the body or limb indicates some form of entrapment, possibly being enslaved to the passions. A snake, or worm, leaving a corpse by its mouth can represent the sexual act, but can also signify the dreamer's control of his or her libido. A snake in the grass denotes disloyalty, trickery and evil.

With its tail in its mouth, this image is one of the oldest available to man and signifies completion, and the union of the spiritual and physical. Being swallowed by a snake shows the need and ability to return to the ultimate, and lose our sense of space and time (*see* **Eating**).

Because snakes are such a low form of life, while also being in some cases poisonous, they have become associated with death and all that man fears. This is symbolised by the mythical figure of Medusa, the snake-haired goddess, who, if looked at directly, would turn men into stone.

A staff or similar object twined around it is also called the caduceus. It signifies that the unconscious forces that are released once the dreamer reconciles the opposing sides of himself create healing, rebirth, and renewal. This is universally represented as two snakes entwined round a central staff and is now known to be a symbolic representation of the basic form of DNA, the 'building blocks' of life. The colours of the snake may give additional insight into the meaning of the dream (*see* **Colours)**.

Snow

Snow represents a crystallisation of an idea. If the snow is melting, then this could suggest the idea or project is fading away, but it is more likely to symbolise something different, and that is the softening of the heart. On the emotional front snow can indicate coldness, and it may be that we need to thaw out a bit ourselves.

Soap

In dreams, soap signals the idea of being cleansed. It could be that we need to clean up our act in order to progress. Also, we may feel a sense of having been made dirty by an experience and our dream is alerting us to the fact that we need to deal with it.

South

The South is representative of earthly passion and sensitivity.

Sowing

Sowing can signify the sexual act, as well as suggesting good tillage. It can also represent the beginning of a new project. We need to decide what is relevant. Sowing in another sense suggests creating the correct environment in which growth can take place. It is the creative act.

Space

If we are aware of space, then we are in touch with our potential for learning – but we may need the space to carry out the process. An acknowledgement of space can also broaden our current view of the world.

Spark

A spark in a dream represents a beginning. It is a small thing that gives rise to a much bigger picture. It can be perceived as our creative potential. A spark can suggest fire and from there love – so look closely, as we don't want to extinguish a potential match!

Spear

The phallic imagery of the spear relates to the masculine. A great warrior holding a spear is a more aggressive male image. The spear is also that part of ourselves which is fertile and dominant. Whether in a man's or a woman's dream, it allows us to be conscious of the need to get straight to the point.

Spectacles – *see* Glasses

Speed

Speed in dreams identifies an intensity of feelings that is not usually available in waking life. Travelling at speed suggests trying to achieve a fast result. Speeding – as in a traffic offence – suggests being too focused on an end result, and not the method of getting there.

Sphinx

A sphinx symbolises some kind of mysterious, enigmatic feeling. The sphinx also stands for vigilance, power and wisdom, as well as dignity.

Spider

The spider, via the horror movie and its scuttling movement, is associated with all things scary and in dreams we can add deviousness to that list. More positively a spider can represent a perfectly woven pattern that both nurtures and protects us.

Spine – *see* Back and backbone *under* Body

Spiral – *see* Shapes

Spire

To see a spire is to recognise a landmark. In previous times, people used the church as a meeting place. Now the pub tends to be a marker, but in dreams the spire still persists in the communal sense of recognition.

Splinter

A splinter can symbolise a minor irritation. Of greater significance is the suggestion that splinters represent painful words or ideas. If we sense we are part of a splinter group, then we are saying to ourselves that it is alright to break away from conventional or mainstream thinking.

Spring

Springtime indicates new growth and opportunity. Now could be the time to set in motion some idea or project that has been hanging around in your mind. Spring is a symbol of progression, particularly insofar as emotion is concerned. We can make a new beginning. A metal spring can signify a huge leap forward.

Square – *see* Shapes

Squirrel

The squirrel represents the possessive aspects of our personalities but may also suggest our ability to guard for the future.

Stab – *see also* Knife

To be stabbed in a dream indicates we are open to being hurt. To stab someone is, conversely, being prepared to hurt. Since a stab wound is penetrative it obviously has connections with aggressive masculine sexuality, but also with the faculty of being able to get straight to the point. When we make ourselves vulnerable we are open to being hurt. Often a stab is a quick way of achieving a result.

Staff

A staff signifies support – that is, the support we need to help us through life. It symbolises the journeying and pilgrimage we must undertake in order to progress. We will not have to do it alone – we shall receive help in some way.

Stage

'All the world's the stage', so to dream of one indicates that we want to make ourselves more visible or known to the world – maybe we have envisaged our potential to succeed; if so, play on.

Stake

To have a stake in something is to have made a commitment, either on a material or emotional level. On another level, the stake is also a symbol of torture or death by fire.

Stairs/Steps

Stairs or steps are often an indication of the efforts we must take in order to achieve a goal. Climbing the stairs is illustrative of the effort that we must make in order to have access to the more mystical, spiritual side of our being. It can more simply be the exertion we practise in everyday life. To have access to the hidden, unconscious side of ourselves, we need to 'go down' into the unconscious, thus going downstairs.

A golden staircase is such a basic image, with so many interpretations, that particular attention needs to be paid to other aspects of the dream, and also the dreamer's spiritual state at that specific time. Largely it represents a 'death', though not necessarily a physical one. It is more the realisation that we no longer need to be trapped within ordinary everyday life, but can move towards a more fulfiling life. It is often interpreted as meaning a way out of the mundane.

Star – *see* **Shapes**

Statue

Dreaming of a statue is to be linking with the unresponsive, cold side of human nature. However, the statue may stand for an ideal, so we must identify what that is by taking in its surroundings and its contours – if possible.

Stealing – *see also* **Thief**

To dream of stealing suggests just that: that we are taking something without permission. We could be taking advantage unfairly. If someone we don't know is stealing from us, it is likely to symbolise a part of ourselves that we don't trust.

'Stealing' is an emotive word, and it will depend on the dreamer's background as to how they feel about inappropriate behaviour. For this image also comes up when dealing with the emotions. Just as an example, a 'needy' person may feel they are stealing affection.

Steeple – *see* **Spire**

Sterilisation

For a woman to dream of being sterilised, either by an operation or otherwise, may be associated with her feeling of powerlessness. In a man's dream sterilisation may suggest sexual dissatisfactions or doubts about his self-image. Sterilisation can also have ambivalent symbolism. It can either suggest cleanliness of spirit, or an aspect of the self that is unable to grow.

Stone

Dreaming of stone can suggest stability but without feeling. Stone has many connotations on an emotional level. For stone to be broken up signifies being badly hurt. Being turned to stone would suggest that we have had to harden up our attitudes.

Being stoned could have two meanings depending on our lifestyle. One interpretation is that we are being punished for misdemeanours; the other is being under the influence of marijuana.

Stork
The stork is a symbol of new life and new beginnings.

Storm – *see also* **Lightning** *and* **Thunder**
A storm indicates an emotional outburst stemming possibly from anger rather than, say, frustration. When we are in difficulty in a relationship, a storm can bring release. When an argument is not appropriate in everyday life, in dreams a storm can represent the clearing of our 'emotional air'.

Strangle
To dream of strangling someone is an attempt to stifle the emotions. To dream of being strangled is to be aware of the need to get a grip on ourselves. Strangulation suggests a violent act of suppression. Emotionally, our more aggressive side may not allow us to act appropriately in certain situations.

Suffocating
When we feel we are suffocating in a dream, it may be that our own fears – possibly of sexual and personal relationships – are threatening to overwhelm us. It can also indicate that we are not in control of our own environment. To be suffocating another person may mean we are overpowering them in real life.

Suicide
Dreaming of suicide alerts us to a violent end to something, perhaps a business project or relationship. Primarily, it is also a sign of anger against the Self. Emotionally, when dreams of suicide occur, we may have come to the end of our ability to cope with a particular situation in our lives. We should be careful not to let it overwhelm us.

Summer
To be conscious of summertime in a dream indicates the good times in our lives – and we may even be able to look forward to success around us. Summer also suggests the potential to relax and take it easy for a while.

Sun

The sun in dreams suggests happiness, warmth and conscious awareness. If we are staring at the sun, then this is said to be symbolic of obsession, but also of worship. With its many seeds, the sunflower represents fertility. In another variation, if we are taking part in a sun dance, then we are, in effect, using the energy of the sun for guidance and vitality.

Swallow

The swallow seen in a dream signifies the coming of Spring and therefore new beginnings.

Swallowing

Swallowing in a dream indicates we are taking something in, perhaps knowledge or information, though if we find it is hard to swallow then this shows we are blocked in some way. Swallowing can also suggest suppressed emotion.

Swan

The swan is the soul of man and is often taken to be the divine bird. It can sometimes denote a peaceful death.

Sweets – *see* Food

Swimming – *see also* Drowning

In dreams, swimming in water is symbolic of the emotions. However, there are different variations; to be swimming upstream would indicate that the dreamer is going against their own nature. Swimming fish can have the same symbolism as sperm, and therefore can indicate the desire for a child. Swimming in clear water indicates being cleansed, whereas dark water could symbolise the possibility of depression.

Sword

A sword can suggest a powerful weapon, but it also indicates strength, courage and justice. For the image of a sword to appear in a dream points to an element of warrior in us, and that we are prepared to fight for our beliefs.

Table

A table as a focus for a meeting is recognised in dreams as a symbol of decision making. As a place for a family gathering, the dreamer may consider meals to be an important ritual. To dream of tidying a table shows we wish to instil a sense of order in our lives. It represents our ability to create order out of chaos. On another level a table can represent judgement and legislation.

Tablet

As with the Tablets of Moses, there is access to esoteric and magical knowledge. Taking or being given tablets in dreams suggests the need to be healthy. If we are giving tablets to someone else we may be aware that their needs – or that part of ourselves represented by them – are not being satisfied.

Tadpole

In a woman's dream tadpoles may signify either her wish, or her ability, to become pregnant. Spiritually, the tadpole represents the Germ of Life and so dreaming of tadpoles links to a focus on the simplicity of life, and perhaps the beginning of a new phase.

Talisman

Man has a deep connection with objects he believes to be sacred, and which are a protection against evil or difficulty. Throughout history, in most pagan religions, objects such as stones and drawings have been given special powers. While consciously the dreamer may not believe in such matters, unconsciously he is capable of linking with ancient magic, so dreaming of a talisman can suggest that his own mental powers are not sufficiently strong to protect him from fear and doubt. He is in need of external help.

Tame

To dream of taming an animal indicates our ability to control or develop a relationship with the animal aspect of ourselves. To dream of being tamed, as though we ourselves are the animal signifies the need for restraint in our lives. To find that something is tame – in the sense of appearing dull or half hearted – suggests that we should reconsider the way we live our lives.

Another symbol is of self- control – in C.S. Lewis' Narnian chronicles Aslan, the Great Lion, despite not being tame, displayed self-control and discipline, and thus ruled with the same. For us, in order to progress, we must do the same.

Tangled

Sometimes when we are confused in everyday life, we may dream of an object being entangled with something else. Often the way that we untangle the object indicates the action we should take. When something like hair is tangled, we need to be aware that our public image is coming across to other people as distorted.

Tank

Dreaming of a water tank is putting ourselves in touch with our inner feelings and emotions. Dreaming of a war or military tank connects us with our own need to defend ourselves, but to be aggressive at the same time. Such a dream would indicate that we are feeling threatened in some way. Often in dreams we become aware of our need to overcome objections and difficulties – the image of a war tank helps to highlight our ability to do this without being hurt.

Tap

A tap symbolises our ability to make use of worldly resources. If we dream of not being able to turn a tap on or off, then this alerts us to our ability – or lack of ability – in controlling things we consider to be ours by right. It may also indicate our need to deal with our emotions in a more appropriate way.

Tapestry – *see* Weaving

Tar

Road tar suggests that we may be trapped somehow, while on the move. Beach tar indicates that we have allowed our emotions to be contaminated. Despite its blackness, tar is not wholly negative; it can also symbolise repair and protection.

Target

Dreaming of a target indicates that we have a goal to aim for. To be shooting at a bull's eye could be interpreted as a search for perfection. To be aiming at a person could suggest either hatred or sexual desire. If we were setting someone else a target in dreams, we would need to understand that the other person in the dream is a reflection of part of ourselves.

Tax

In dreams having to pay a tax suggests some kind of a penalty for living the lifestyle we have chosen for ourselves. Different taxes have different symbolism. Thus, dreaming of car tax would indicate that greater effort is needed to move forward. To be paying income tax suggests that we may feel we owe a debt to society. To be paying council tax may suggest that we feel we have to pay for the 'space' in which we exist. Refusing to pay any taxes suggests an unwillingness to conform. Any tax levied in a dream indicates we are aware of our responsibilities.

Teacher

A teacher is an authority figure – often the first one we meet outside the family. It may be that we are looking for guidance, or an alternative guidance, as the teacher's views are often different from those we may get at home.

Tears

If we are crying in a dream, then it may be that in normal life we find it difficult to show our emotions. To dream of being in tears and then to wake up and discover that we are actually crying, suggests that some hurt or trauma has come sufficiently close to the surface to enable us to deal with it on a conscious level.

Teasing

To be teased in a dream indicates that our behaviour in everyday life may not be wholly appropriate. If we are teasing someone and pointing out their idiosyncrasies, we may actually be highlighting our own discrepancies. Teasing can also come about because of insecurity and an awareness of our own doubts and fears.

Teeth – *See* Body

Telegram

Receiving a telegram in a dream highlights communication in the most efficient way possible under the circumstances. It indicates that a part of ourselves is attempting to give us information in a way that is going to be remembered. If we send a telegram, then we want known something about ourselves that we cannot impart verbally. On another level, a telegram symbolises the way we make knowledge tangible.

Telephone

The telephone in a dream connects us with contact and communication – either with another person or with a part of ourselves. Being contacted by telephone suggests there is information available to us that we do not already know. If we recognise the number we are ringing, then obviously we may need to contact that person or establishment. If we are looking for a telephone number we are undecided about future actions.

Telescope

Using a telescope in a dream suggests that we are taking a closer look at something. A telescope enhances our view and makes it bigger and wider. We do need to make sure, however, that we are not taking a one-sided view of things. On another plane, a telescope can symbolise clairvoyance.

Temple – *see also* Churches *under* Religious Imagery

A temple can often symbolise our own body – we need to treat it with care and respect, or suffer the consequences. There may also be a sense of awe attached to the creative elements of a temple.

Tenant
To have a tenant signifies that we are prepared to have someone live in our space. If we are tenants, then we need to be taking more responsibility. On a commercial level it may be an insight into how to handle a transaction.

Tent
A tent in a dream would suggest that we feel we are on the move, and not able to settle down and put down roots. We perhaps need to get away from everyday responsibilities for a time. There is benefit to be gained by being self-sufficient and not dependent on anyone – we are not tied to any one place, but can be where we need to be at short notice.

Tests – *see also* Exams
Dreaming of tests of any sort can indicate some form of self-assessment. Medical tests may be alerting us to the need to watch our health. A driving test would suggest a test of confidence or ability, whereas a written test would signify a test of knowledge.

Testing something in a dream suggests that there has been some form of standard set, to which we feel we must adhere. This need not mean that we are setting ourselves against others, but simply that we have resolved to maintain a certain standard.

Text
For a text to appear in a dream would signify the need for encouragement and perhaps wisdom. Text from a book or a text of a play would indicate the need for the dreamer to carry out instructions in a particular way in order to achieve success. On another plane, a spiritual text is an encouraging message to enable us to progress.

Thaw
In dreams to be aware of a thaw is to note a change in our own emotional responses. If we are aware of coldness within ourselves, on an emotional level we need to discover what the problem is or was, and why we have reacted as we did. In another way a thaw can suggest the ability to come to terms with old barriers and to become warm and loving.

Theatre – *See* **Stage**

Thief
Dreaming of a thief links with our fear of losing things, or of having them taken away. It may be love, it may be possessions. When a thief appears in dreams, we are aware of part of our personality which can waste our own time and energy on meaningless activity. A spiritual thief is that part of us which has no respect for our beliefs.

Thigh – *see* **Limbs** *under* **Body**

Third Eye – *see* **Religious Imagery**

Thirst
We need to satisfy an inner need – it may be that we have been feeling low and need a boost. Also if we need to satisfy a thirst, then this translates to satisfying a desire. If we are thirsty in a dream, we need to look very carefully at either what we are being denied, or what we are denying ourselves, in waking life.

Thorn
To dream of being pierced by a thorn signifies that a minor difficulty has got through our defences. If the thorn draws blood, we need to look at what is happening in our lives that could make us vulnerable. In a woman's dream this could represent the sexual act, or rather, fear of intercourse. A thorn also represents suffering, particularly a physical suffering.

Thread
A thread symbolises a line of thinking or an enquiry of some kind, probably regarding the way our lives are going. If we are threading a needle, besides the obvious sexual representation, it can also relate to incompetence – many of us know how difficult it is to thread a needle.

Threshold
Crossing the threshold in dreams indicates that new experiences and new

responsibilities are on the horizon. Being lifted across a threshold may suggest marriage, or in this day and age, merely a new relationship.

Throat – *see* **Body**

Throne
When we dream of sitting on a throne, we are acknowledging our right to take authority. When the throne is empty, we are not prepared to accept the responsibility for who we are. It may be that we are conscious of a lack of parenting. When someone else is on the throne, we may have passed over authority to that person. In dreams a throne can represent our ability to belong to groups, or to society. We often use word play or slang in interpretation, but in this case it is unlikely that the throne relates to the lavatory.

Thumb – *see* **Body**

Thunder/Thunderbolts – *see also* **Storm**
If we hear thunder in a dream, then it is a warning of some emotional storm to come. If the thunder is in the distance, then there is still time to compose ourselves and ride out any anger we may have. Thunder also has the potential to cleanse.

Tiara – *see* **Crown**

Tide – *see also* **Sea**
We need to go with the ebb and flow of life and emotions a bit more. A high tide may symbolise high energy, whereas a low tide would suggest a drain on our abilities or energy.

Timber – *see* **Wood**

Titans
Titans in dreams appear as huge, over bearing god-like figures. In this context they represent the forces within us that allow things to manifest, or to happen. There are titanic forces that can arise in dreams: they are

those parts of us that are untamed and untameable. When used properly, they are the ability to create a world of our own.

Toad
Implicit in the ugliness of the toad is the power of mutation and growth into something beautiful. To dream of toads is to connect with whatever the dreamer may consider ugly in life, yet also to recognise the power of transformation. For a toad and an eagle to appear is to note the difference between earthly and spiritual values.

Tobacco
If the dreamer is a smoker, then tobacco suggests a way of comforting ourselves. If not, then the symbolism is more to do with being able to achieve a certain state of mind – possibly a mood lift or a more relaxed outlook.

Toilet
There has always been the inevitable association with sexuality. Nowadays, though, the symbolism is more to do with notions of privacy, and the ability to reach a state where we can release our feelings in private. If there is something wrong with the toilet, then we are emotionally blocked. Going to an unfamiliar toilet suggests we are in a position where we do not know what the outcome to a situation will be. Cleaning a dirty toilet suggests we are losing our 'prudish' attitude.

Tomb
If we sense that we are a tomb raider, then we are entering the darker parts of our personality. If we are trapped in a tomb in a dream we may be trapped by fear, pain or old outdated attitudes in our waking life. If there are bodies in the tomb, these are usually parts of ourselves we have either not developed or have killed off.

Tongue – *see* Body

Tools
Tools suggest the practical tools we have at our disposal for enhancing

our lifestyle. Each tool will have its own significance. A drill suggests working through emotions and fears as well as attitudes that have become hardened. A hammer provides the energy to break down old patterns of behaviour and resistances. A saw suggests being able to cut through all the rubbish we have accumulated in order to make something new.

Top
To be at the top is to have succeeded in our objective, usually after effort. To be on top is to have accepted leadership. Trying to reach the top suggests greater exertion is required.

Torch
In dreams, a torch can depict self-confidence. It can also suggest the need to be able to move forward. A torch can be used not only for ourselves, but also for other people. Dreaming of a torch shows we can have the confidence to know that because of our own knowledge we have the ability to see the way forward. On another level we may feel that we need spiritual guidance, and this can sometimes be symbolised as a torch.

Tornado – *see* Storm

Torpedo
The torpedo is often connected to aggressive male sexuality. A torpedo also suggests a way of directing energy – this may be a type of honesty in getting to the point that we can do with friends, or it may be a warning that such directness could be harmful.

Torture
When an image connected with torture appears in a dream, often we are trying to come to terms with a great hurt. This does not need to be on a physical level it is more likely to be emotional or mental pain.

Totem/Totem Pole
A totem pole appearing in a dream links us with a very basic, primitive need for protection. A totem pole is also believed to have a strength and power of its own. When it appears in dreams we need to be looking at

those parts of our lives that are based around our belief system, to find out if we are really living according to those beliefs.

Tower (obelisk, steeple, lighthouse, etc.)

Any image of a tower is representative of the personality, and the Soul within. While there are obvious connotations that connect it with masculinity, it is more correct to perceive it as the Self within a wider context. When thought of in this way, attention can then be paid to other attributes of the tower, such as where windows, doors and staircases are placed. This leads to a greater understanding of the Spiritual self.

Track – *see* Path *and* Train

Traffic accidents and offences

These may all be to do with sexuality or self-image, or the way we handle aggression or carelessness, both in ourselves and others. A collision might suggest, therefore, a conflict with someone. Road rage would signify not being in control of our emotions. Avoiding an accident would typify being able to control our impulses.

Train

A train, as a method of public transport, brings the dreamer's attitude to social behaviour and relationships into prominence and elucidates his attitude to himself. A steam train would denote outdated and obsolete behaviour, whereas a modern-day train might suggest speed and efficiency. A tube train may indicate exploring the unconscious.

We have successfully achieved a particular goal and circumstances have gone our way when we dream of actually catching the train. If we miss the train, however, we may be missing an opportunity and do not have the resources to enable us to succeed. Equally we may feel that external circumstances are imposing an element of control over us. Often dreams of missing a train and then in the same dream catching either it or a later one, suggest that we are managing our inner resources better. Dreams of missing a train alternating with dreams of catching one show that the dreamer is trying to sort out his motivation. Getting off the train before its destination means that we are afraid of succeeding at a particular project. This can also signify premature ejaculation. Getting off the train before it starts suggests the dreamer has changed his mind about a situation in waking life.

Traitor

To dream of a traitor suggests that one is subconsciously aware of deviousness. This may be in someone else, or it could be a part of our personality that is letting us down. We may feel that our standards are not appreciated by others. When in a dream we are betrayed by others and believe them to have let us down, we are perhaps aware of the fact that it is through shared belief in waking life that they have let us down. This would mean they are traitors.

Transparent

If something appears transparent, then it may be that we are feeling vulnerable – though we may also be able to see things more clearly. Also, transparency can indicate an honesty and openness within us.

Transport

The transport we are using in our dreams may suggest how we are moving through this specific period of our lives. Previously the horse was used as an image to depict how we dealt with life. Nowadays the car, the aeroplane and so on have been substituted. The vehicle which appears in our dreams often conforms with the view we hold of ourselves. For instance, we may be driving a very basic type of car or a Rolls Royce. We may be driving a work-day vehicle or a sports car. Such an image may represent either our physical body or our personality. If the dreamer is with friends the suggestion is that he or she may wish to look at group goals. If he does not know the other people he may need to explore his ability to make social relationships.

Transvestism – *see* Sex

Trap/Trapped

To be in a trap in a dream signifies that we feel we are trapped by outside circumstances. To be aware of trapping something or someone is attempting to hold on to them. When we feel trapped in dreams, we are not usually able to break free of old patterns of thought and behaviour – we may need outside help. On another plane, it may suggest that we are holding ourselves back.

Treasure – *see also* Jewels

Treasure represents what we value – often something that we have achieved through hard work and effort. To find a box that has treasure in it is to have some understanding of the fact that we must break through limitations before we find what we are looking for.

Tree

The tree is symbolic in dreams of the basic structure of our inner lives. Different trees represent different things. For example, a tree with wide branches would suggest a warm loving personality, whereas a small close-leafed tree would suggest an uptight personality. As far as the roots of a tree are concerned, this is connected to how we relate to the earth. On the other hand, the trunk of a tree indicates how we may use all available energies. In another sense a tree represents heaven, earth and water – the Tree of Life.

Trespassing

When we find ourselves trespassing in a dream, we are perhaps intruding on someone's personal space, or allowing them to intrude on ours. This may also suggest that there is a part of ourselves that is private and feels vulnerable. We should respect those boundaries. On a spiritual level we are perhaps approaching areas of knowledge where we cannot go without permission.

Triangle – *see* Shapes

Trophy

If we dream of a trophy, then we are recognising that we have done something that deserves a reward. A cup suggests receptivity, whereas a shield indicates protection. A trophy may also signify that we need to, or about to, achieve a goal.

Trumpet

A trumpet suggests either a warning or a 'call to arms'. When we have conflict around us, for example, a trumpet is often the symbol that appears. A trumpet can also suggest the need to maximise our potential.

Trunk

A trunk could represent a long journey; however, it is more likely to symbolise old ideas. A trunk also signifies that it is time to sort out any physical or mental rubbish we may have stored.

Tunnel

A tunnel in a dream represents the need to explore our own unconscious, and those things we have left untouched. If there is a light at the end of the tunnel, it indicates we are reaching the final stages of our exploration. If something is blocking the tunnel, some past fear or experience is stopping us from progressing. A tunnel can also symbolise the birth canal and therefore the process of birth. In another sense the image of a tunnel helps us to escape from the unconscious into the light, and also to go down into the depths.

Turf

To dream of being on 'sacred' turf – ground that is revered because of its association, such as Wembley, Lords etc. – is to wish for supreme success. Dreaming of one's association with a particular piece of ground can activate certain memories and feelings connected with happy times. This may, by recollection, help to clarify a particular problem or situation.

Twins

In dreams twins may, if known to us, simply be themselves. If they are not known to us, then they may represent two sides of one idea. Often in everyday life, we come up against conflicts between two opposites. Twins in dreams can actually represent two sides of our personality acting in harmony. Duality must eventually reunite into unity. Twins illustrate the idea that while there is separation at the moment, unity can be achieved.

Umbilical

The Silver Cord is the spiritual connection seen psychically as the connection between body and soul. In dreams it is often experienced as the umbilical cord, signifying life giving connections. Teenagers often dream of severing the umbilical cord as they grow into adulthood. When we have perhaps not yet learnt to take care of our own needs in a mature way and have an emotional dependency on others, the umbilical cord in dreams can signify that dependency.

Under/Underneath

Being underneath something signifies taking shelter or submitting to someone else's handling of a situation. It may also represent the part of us that we conceal, or the part that is less capable, and perhaps more vulnerable.

Underground

The subconscious or the unconscious is often perceived in dreams as a cave or place underground. Dreams give us opportunities to explore our own hidden depths. To dream of being underground will often allow us to come to terms with that side in a very easy way. To dream of being on the underground or subway usually signifies the journeys we are prepared (or forced) to take towards understanding ourselves.

Undress

To be undressing in a dream suggests a need for spiritual openness and honesty, but can also suggest that we may be putting ourselves in touch with our own sexual feelings. When we find ourselves undressing in a dream, we may also be needing to reveal our true feelings about a situation around us, and to have the freedom to be totally open about those feelings.

Unemployment
Dreaming of being unemployed suggests that we are not making the best use of our talents, or that we feel our talents are not being recognised. It can indicate that we feel inadequate.

Unicorn
When a unicorn appears in a dream, we are linking with the innocent, pure part of ourselves. This is the instinctive, receptive feminine principle. There is a story that unicorns missed being taken into Noah's Ark because they were too busy playing. We need to be mindful of what is going on in the real world if we are to survive.

University
Dreaming of being in a university highlights our own individual potential and learning ability. Since a university is a place of 'higher' learning, we are being made aware of the breadth of experience and increase in knowledge available to us. We need to move away from the mundane and ordinary into specific areas of knowledge and awareness.

Up, upper
We have the proficiency to be able to achieve much. We are capable of getting the 'upper hand' (gaining supremacy) in whatever situation the dream refers to. We can move away from the mundane, ordinary, everyday world, and learn to win.

Urine – *see* Body

Urn – *see also* Vase

For many people the tea urn is a symbol of community life. To dream of one suggests our ability to belong to a community and act for the greater good. Just as all receptacles signify the feminine principle, so does the urn, although in a more ornate form. In earlier times, a draped urn signified death. That symbolism is still carried on today in the urn used in crematoriums. Thus, to dream of an urn may alert us to our feelings about death.

Valley

There are two meanings which can be given to the image of a valley. The first is the fairly obvious one of the sheltering, more nurturing side of our personalities – usually associated with the feminine: the second is the valley of death, a transition period between two states of being. This may represent a need to explore our unconscious selves or the lesser known parts of ourselves.

Vampire

Life threatening evil or negative influences can be represented by the vampire in dreams. When heavy demands are made on us we are figuratively being 'sucked dry.'

Often the fear of emotional and sexual relationships can be represented in dreams as a vampire. Ancient symbols that have represented such fear of the unknown can still appear in dreams. The succubus and incubus preying on young people's vital energy is often pictured as a vampire.

Vase

As a holder of beautiful things, any receptacle – such as a vase, water pot, pitcher or urn – tends to represent the feminine within a dream, the accepting and receptive nature of the feminine, intuitive side. Such an object can also signify the Great Mother and hence, by association, creativity.

Vault

A vault represents the meeting place of the spiritual and physical. Consequently, a vault also symbolises death. While a vault *can* represent a tomb, it also represents the 'archives' or records to which we all have access. In dreams, any dark, hidden place suggests sexual potency or the unconscious. It can also symbolise our store of personal resources, those things we learn as we grow and mature.

VD – *see* **Sex**

Vegetables – *see* **Food** *and* **Harvest**

Vegetation – *see* **Plants**

Veil
A veil in a dream suggests the Occult or some kind of secret which we are hiding from ourselves. It may be something of which consciously we are ignorant but which with a little delving can be revealed.

Velvet
There are two very distinct meanings which can be attributed to velvet: the ancient one which signifies discord, and the modern day which suggests softness and sensuousness. It can also mean richness and giftedness.

Vermin
In the sense that they are unwanted and invade others' space vermin represent a negativity that needs to be got rid of.

Vertical
The vertical in dreams tends to represent the spiritual realm. The points of the compass appearing in dreams can give some indication of where we are spiritually (see individual listings of compass points).

Vicar – *see* **Authority Figures**

Vice
The side of ourselves which is rebellious and out of step with society may allow us to behave in dreams in ways which are not those we would normally try in waking life. We may in both cases need to make adjustments in our behaviour. Conversely, sloth, envy, apathy, etc. in one

of our dream characters may enable us to handle that tendency within ourselves. Dreaming of a vice in the sense of something which grips, suggests some kind of constraint in our lives.

Victim
If the dreamer is repressing his own ability to develop spiritual potential, he will appear in a dream as a victim – a victim of his own making. The nature of the difficulty may reveal itself through the dream content. In dreams we are often aware of something happening to us over which we have no control, or some way in which we are creating a no-win situation.

Violence
Any violence in dreams is a reflection of our own inner feeling, sometimes about ourselves, sometimes about the situations around us. Often the type of violence is worthy of notice if we are fully to understand ourselves.

Viper – *see* Serpent *and* Snake

Virgin
Spiritually, innocence and purity can often be dedicated to service. The virginal mind – that is, a mind that is free from deception and guile – is perhaps more important than physically being a virgin, and it is this aspect which often becomes evident in dreams. In a woman's dream such a figure suggests she is in touch with her own psyche.

Virgin Mother – *see* Religious Imagery

Visit
One's spiritual guide often first makes itself available by a visit in the dream state. To be visited by someone in a dream can suggest that there is information, warmth or love available to us and that we should be receptive to it. To be paying someone else a visit in a dream signifies that we may need to widen our horizons in some fashion in order to lead a fuller life.

Voice

A voice that speaks through or to one has two types of meaning. If one believes in the spirit realm, this is communication from a discarnate spirit. More psychologically, when we suppress certain parts of our personalities, they may surface in dreams as disembodied voices.

Void – *see* Abyss

Volcano

An erupting volcano usually signifies that we are not in control of a situation or of our emotions – of which there may be a hurtful release. If the lava is more prominent, feelings will run very deep. If the lava has cooled there has been a deep passion which has now cooled off. If the explosiveness is more noticeable, anger may be more prominent. To dream of a volcano being extinct can indicate either that we have 'killed off' our passions, or that a difficult situation has come to an end.

Vomiting

Vomiting is a symbol of a discharge of evil. To dream of vomiting suggests a discharge of disagreeable feelings and emotions. It is a clearing of something within that makes us extremely uncomfortable. When we become overloaded, we may need to 'throw up' the distress it is causing.

Vote

When we have given unconditional acceptance to something, we have placed our trust in it. To vote for something in dreams may suggest that we believe wholeheartedly in a particular cause, or are becoming conscious of our need to belong to a group of like-minded people.

Vow

A vow is a pact or agreement between two people or oneself and God, or more correctly a spiritual promise made between the dreamer and his universe. To dream of making a vow is to be recognising responsibility for one's own life. It is more binding than a simple promise and the results are more far-reaching. It is an inner acknowledgement of the way we wish to be.

Wading

Spiritually, wading, particularly through water, suggests a cleansing process which ties in with baptism. It can often allow us to understand what our emotions can do to us, how they can stop us from moving forward, or how we can work with the flow. Moving through any other substance can suggest how we tend to impede our own progress – we can literally get bogged down.

Wafer

The Body of Christ, the Bread of Life, is represented in Christian communion services by a wafer – a thin layer of matter which is usually very fragile. Thus in dreams a wafer represents something which is easily broken and which we need to treat with respect.

Wages

Spiritually, wages can represent payment for our actions, and the recompense we deserve coming our way. Often, when we are doing something that we do not want to do – or which we do not enjoy – the only pay-off is in the 'wages' we receive. To receive a wage packet suggests that our value is tied up with other things such as loyalty and duty.

Wailing

Grieving and the making of sounds is used spiritually to banish bad spirits, or to summon the spirits and to get in touch with a power that is greater than ourselves. Wailing is a prolonged way of releasing emotions. Through dreams we can often put ourselves in touch with emotions which we might not otherwise allow ourselves to access in ordinary life.

Waiting

To be waiting for somebody, or something, in a dream, implies a need to recognise the importance of patience. We must wait for the passage of time. We may be looking to other people, or outside circumstances, to help us move forward or make decisions. If *we* are impatient, it may be that our expectations are too high.

Wake

A wake, in the sense of a funeral service, gives us an opportunity to grieve appropriately. If in dreams we find ourselves attending such an occasion, there may be some reason in our lives for us to go through a period of grieving, or we may need support to overcome a disappointment. We need to let go those things which we hold dear.

Walking

In a dream, walking indicates the way in which we should be moving forward, a journey of exploration. Walking purposefully suggests we know where we are going. To be wandering aimlessly suggests we need to create goals for ourselves. To take pleasure in the act of walking is to return to the innocence of the child, or to obtain relief from stress. To be using a walking stick is to recognise our need for support and assistance.

Wallet

In dreams, the wallet is a representation of how we look after our resources. These need not simply be financial resources, but can be of any kind. Many dreams can suggest our attitude to money, and to dream of a wallet is one of those dreams.

Interestingly, because the wallet can also take on the significance of a container, it suggests the feminine aspects of care and containment, and highlights our attitude to intuition and awareness.

Wallpaper

Wallpaper often symbolises an outer facade of some kind. To be putting up wallpaper signifies covering up the old self (possibly superficially), particularly if the old wallpaper is not removed. To be stripping wallpaper in dreams suggests stripping away the old facade in order to create a new image. We may be wanting to make changes in our lives but need to experiment – and get a proper fit – first.

Walls

A wall signifies a block to progress. The nature of the wall will give some clue as to what the block is. Construction or demolition of a wall or building suggests that we all have the ability within us to construct successful lives, and equally an ability to self-destruct. A dream that highlights construction or demolition gives us access to those qualities and abilities within ourselves. For instance, an old wall suggests an old problem, whereas a glass wall would indicate difficulties with perception. A dream where walls close in could describe the remembered feelings of birth, but is more likely to represent a feeling of being trapped by the lifestyle we have. A brick wall, rampart, or dividing wall all signify the difference between two states of reality, often the inner psychological state and the exterior everyday world.

Waltz – *see* Dance

Wand

To dream of a wand can symbolise 'magical' powers which may influence us. We are aware of some force external to ourselves which needs harnessing. When we dream of using a wand we are aware of our influence over others. Conversely, if someone else uses a wand we are aware of the power of suggestion, either for negative or for positive within a situation in our lives.

War

In dreams war always denotes conflict of one form or another; it is a way of dealing with distress and disorder. The outcome should be the re-establishment of order, although sometimes this can only happen through the passage of time. To dream of war, therefore, indicates that this natural process is taking place on an inner level. There is some kind of conflict, which may be going on inwardly, but may well have been deliberately engineered rather than spontaneous. We need to be more conscious of the effect our actions will have on others.

Warmth

A feeling of warmth in a dream can symbolise unconditional love. It touches our 'feel good' factor and enhances our sense of comfort and well being. Psychologically, feelings of cheerfulness and hopefulness can create an awareness of warmth and can be interchangeable.

Warning
To be warning someone highlights our ability to be aware of difficulty and danger, either to others or to hidden parts of our personality. To receive a warning in a dream suggests that we are aware that either internally or externally something needs attention. We may be putting ourselves in danger. The environment within the dream may clarify this. To receive a written warning indicates we may be behaving in an inappropriate manner.

Warts
We are often distressed by anything which is out of the ordinary or wrong. Any blemish which comes to the attention in dreams can be accepted as evidence of there being a distortion in our view of ourselves or of the world. A great deal of folklore has grown up around warts and how to get rid of them. Dreaming of warts can connect with that part of ourselves which remains superstitious.

Washing
Since water is a symbol for emotion and the unconscious, washing stands for achieving a relationship with our emotional selves and dealing successfully with the results. Dreaming of washing either oneself or, for instance, clothes, suggests getting rid of negative feelings – our attitude, either internally or externally, needs changing. Washing other people touches on our need to care for others.

Waste
Waste in dreams signifies matter or information we no longer need. It can now be thrown away. Waste can also suggest a misuse of resources – we may, initially, be using too much energy on a particular project, and may need to reassess how we are running our lives.

Watch – *see* Clock

Water

Water is usually taken in dreams to symbolise all that is emotional and feminine. Deep water suggests either being out of our depth, or entering our own subconscious. It also represents cleansing, being able to wash away the things which deeply affect us in everyday life. In baptism, water is a cleanser of previously held 'sins', also often those habits, beliefs and concepts which we have inherited from the family. So, to dream of a baptism, particularly our own, may suggests that it is time to let go of these 'inheritances'.

Water can also stand for the dreamer's potential and his ability to create a new life in response to his own inner urges.

The representation of water appears so often in dreams, with so many different meanings, that it is possible only to suggest some probable ones. Thus coming up out of the water indicates a fresh start whereas deep water suggests the unconscious; flowing water signifies peace and comfort or going with the scheme of events. Going down in water indicates a need to renew one's inner strength, whilst being immersed in water can suggest pregnancy and birth and our feelings about them. while rushing water denotes passion with shallow water reveals a lack of essential energy. To be on the water (as in a boat) can represent indecision or a lack of emotional commitment, while to be in the e water but not moving signifies inertia. (See individual listings for other water-based dreams.)

Waterfall

A waterfall is often taken to represent an orgasm, or any display of emotion that is powerful and yet under control. It can also suggest some kind of spiritual cleansing.

Wax

Wax is symbolic of the need for spiritual pliability, and the desire to move away from rigidity. Dreaming of wax is a great deal to do with the pliability that we are able to achieve in our lives. We should be prepared to give way, but also to be firm when necessary. More negatively, wax can also be taken to represent insincerity, with the ability to be affected by external events, and irrevocably changed.

Wealth – *see also* **Money**

Wealth and status usually go naturally together, so often when we are having problems in dealing with our own status in life we will have dreams about wealth. It can also often indicate the resources that we have or of which we can make use.

Weather

Weather, as being part of the 'environment' of the dream, usually indicates our moods and emotions. We are aware of changing external situations and circumstances and have to be careful to adjust our conduct in response to these. This would suggest that we need to recognise that we are all part of a greater whole rather than individuals in our own right.

Dreaming about the weather can also point to our internal responses to situations. If, for instance, there is a storm in our dream we are, perhaps, angry and aggressive. If we are watching a very blue, unclouded sky, it signifies fair weather and happier times ahead.

Weaving

Weaving is one of the strongest spiritual images. In most cultures there is an image of our fate being woven in a particular pattern. We are not supposed to be in control of that pattern, but must accept that Gods or the gods know what is best. However, it does suggest that we need to take responsibility for our own lives. To be doing any handicraft shows that we have situations in hand.

Weaving as a symbol is taken to signify life itself and dreaming about it often represents our attitude to the way in which we run our lives.

Wedding – *see* **Marriage**

Wedding Ring – *see also* **Ring**

Traditionally, the wedding ring was a symbol of total encircling love. To dream of this symbol is to link in with that basic concept of eternity. Within the human being there is the need to make vows, to give promises and above all to symbolise the making of those promises. To lose or be wearing the ring on any other figure than the third finger of the left hand in a dream suggests difficulties within the relationship.

Weeds – *see also* **Plants**

Weeds, plants which grow on waste ground, may indicate misplaced trust, misplaced energy or even misplaced attempts at success. To be digging up weeds would show that we are aware that it is important to free ourselves of the non essential. Mental attitudes which clog us up and do not allow us to move forward, and old patterns of behaviour, can very often be shown in dreams as weeds. Plants growing wild do have healing properties, and our bodies can often give us information in dreams as to what we need.

Weeping – *see also* **Mourning**

Weeping suggests uncontrollable emotion or grief, so to experience either ourselves or someone else weeping in dreams is to show that there needs to be a discharge of such emotion. We may be mourning some spiritual quality we have lost. We may simply be creating difficulty within ourselves and this enables us to express the feelings we have bottled up.

Something exuding moisture so that it seems to be weeping is often deemed to be miraculous, and this dream can appear quite often in stages of transition as we are moving from one state of awareness to another. The excess energy can be shown as a weeping plant, tree or some such image.

Weighing

To be weighing something in dreams is to be assessing its worth, deciding what is of value to us. Weighing something up is to be trying to make a decision in order to decide what the risks are in any situation. The image of the scales indicates we are looking for justice and balance.

Weight

Weight in a dream indicates gravitas and seriousness and may well indicate the need to be practical and down to earth. Experiencing a weight in a dream is to be conscious of our responsibilities, or those things which are holding us down.

Well

Occasionally there is a degree of wordplay in the image of a well in a dream which suggests our ability to be 'well'. Through our intuitive, aware selves, we contact the depths of our very being and open up the potential for healing and success.

West
The west can symbolise death, but more properly the state after death when there is an increased spiritual awareness. Traditionally, it can also represent the more logical side of our natures.

Wheel – *see also* **Circle** *under* **Shapes**
When we need to make changes and move forward the wheel is an appropriate symbol. It represents the Wheel of Life, and the cycle of growth and decay. When we lose motivation, we may dream of losing a wheel.

Whip/Lash
The whip or lash is an instrument of torture and suggests corrective punishment and self-flagellation. In trying to force things to happen, we may also be creating problems for ourselves, by trying to be either too controlled or controlling. The lash was often used by monks and nuns to mortify the flesh and bring the natural urges into subjection, and in dreams this image may still appear.

Whistle
A whistle blown in a dream can mark the end of a particular phase of time. It can also sound as a warning to make us aware of something such as a deviation or difficulty. As a method of controlling and training, there may be information in the way it is being blown. The whistle may also be seen as a phallic symbol.

Wig
A hairpiece or toupée highlights false ideas or an unnatural attitude. A judge's wig can suggest authority, wisdom and judgement.

Will
At a time when we need everything to be done properly and with a certain degree of precision, to dream of a will – our own or someone else's – is highlighting how our inner self can make us aware of what is

right for us. To be making a will is to be stating our intent, and may also have to do with the way we need to look after those we love. To inherit from a will means that we need to look at the tendencies, idiosyncrasies and beliefs we have inherited from our families.

Making a will is a very final action and in dreams such an act can signify a recognition that we are entering a new phase of life and must clear up the old. There is the obvious play on words, where a will would indicate the will to do or to be – the determination to take action, for instance.

Wind

The power of the Spirit and the movement of Life are often perceived as wind, and in dreams we may recognise a powerful passionate part of ourselves through the symbol of wind. It also represents the intellect and the wisdom we have available to us.

Windmill

As a storehouse of fruitfulness and of conservation, in dreams a windmill can represent the feminine or the mother. The representation of a windmill in dreams also suggests the proper use of resources. Because wind often suggests intellect, it is therefore the use of intellectual assets.

Wine

Wine suggests the potential for spiritual abundance and highlights our capability of using what we harvest to give fun and happiness. We are able to use the sum of our experiences to make something fine and new. A wine cellar thus signifies the totality of our past experiences. A wine bottle is taken to indicate the penis and masculinity, but also to suggest femininity and containment.

The wine glass is interesting in that it can have two meanings. Firstly, it stands for the happiness and joviality of celebration and secondly it can stand for pregnancy. A broken wine glass can depict sorrow, or in a woman's dream, miscarriage.

Wings

Wings, connected with flight and freedom, can also be protective. An angel's wings depict the power to transcend our difficulties, often through the protection of greater knowledge. A broken wing indicates that a previous trauma is preventing us from 'taking off'.

Winter

Within the cycle of nature, winter suggest a time of lying fallow before rebirth; hence winter can also mean death or old age. In dreams, winter can represent a time in our lives which is unfruitful. When we are emotionally cold or lonely, images associated with winter can appear.

In clairvoyance, the seasons can also indicate a time of year when something may happen.

Witness

To be a witness to, for instance, an accident, suggests that we need to observe some circumstance in our life very carefully. We may be being called to account for our actions or beliefs, or our way of looking at things. To be in a witness box suggests that we are accountable to a higher authority.

Wood – *see also* Forest *and* Tree

Dreaming of wood, in the sense of timber, suggests our ability to appreciate the past and to build on what has gone before. If the wood is still standing and growing it is more likely to represent the feminine or fertility. If it is cut timber, then the purpose for which it is being used will be important. We are most likely to need some form of structure or shelter. Wooden toys can indicate our need to be in control of our environment or of our lives. When our behaviour becomes rigid or wooden, dreams will often attempt to make us aware of this and of the necessity to balance our feelings.

Woman

In a woman's dream a female family member or friend is often representative of an aspect of her own disposition, but often one she has not yet fully integrated. In a man's dream such a figure describes his relationship with his own feelings and with his intuitive, softer side. It can denote how he relates to his female partner.

A goddess or holy woman signifies more spiritually the highest aspect of the feminine that can be attained, and the need to work for the greater good. It can also suggest intuitive wisdom.

Oriental women appearing in dreams usually suggest the enigmatic side of the feminine. In a woman's dream they will reveal her own intuitive and exquisite powers. In a man's dream such figures will often reveal his attitude to his own sexuality.

An older woman most often represents the dreamer's mother and her sense of inherited awareness. **An unknown woman** in dreams will represent either the Anima in a man's dream, or the Shadow in a woman's. It is the quality of surprise and intrigue which allows us to explore further the relevance of that figure. We can gain a great deal of information because the figure is unknown, and therefore needs to be carefully considered.

Wool

Wool has from earliest times represented warmth and protectiveness in dreams and is symbolic of spiritual protection. Nowadays it particularly represents gentleness and mothering. The best example of such a dream is that of Alice in *Through the Looking Glass*, when she is aware of the sheep in the boat, knitting.

Worm

At its basic interpretation, the worm can suggest the penis. The worm is not necessarily seen to be particularly clean, but is one of those images which can have several meanings. Depending on the dreamer's attitude to sexuality and gender, there may be a sense of threat to one's self-image, and a sense of ineffectiveness and insignificance.

Being given to the worms is a metaphor for death, so spiritual changes may shortly be taking place. If we are particularly conscious of a wormcast, that is, the earth the worm has passed through its body, then this is a transformation image and indicates we are capable of changing our lives into something more fertile.

Worship – *see also* Religious Imagery

An act of worship is an acknowledgement of the power that belief has. Dreaming of being in a situation where we are worshipping an idea, a person, a concept or an object is to be opening ourselves up to its influence. If we are not particularly religious but find ourselves in the middle of such an act, we may be trying to decide how best to function in a group or team of people.

To be worshipping an object which is not a religious image may suggest that we are paying too much attention to whatever that object represents, and giving too much importance to a particular area of our lives. For instance we may be too materialistic or be paying too much attention to sex and so on.

Wound

A wound symbolises an experience – which was probably unpleasant – that the dreamer should take note of and learn from. The type of wound will be important in interpreting the dream. A large ugly wound will suggest more violence, whereas a small one may indicate that there has been a more focused attack.

Any wound or trauma in dreams will signify hurt feelings or emotions. If we are inflicting the wounds our own aggressive behaviour is being drawn to our attention; if the wounds are being inflicted on us we may be making ourselves into, or being, the victim.

Wreath

A wreath in dreams can have the same significance as any of the binding symbols such as harnesses and halters. It forms a bond which cannot be broken, or a sacrifice which must be accepted. So, to receive a funeral wreath would suggest the ending, perhaps of a relationship, but also its continuation in a different form. Years ago a wreath in a dream could also suggest honour.

Wreck

A wreck of some kind symbolises a failure, possibly through lack of control. The dreamer will have to rescue the situation and struggle through to reach his goal. Dreaming of a wreck, such as a car or shipwreck, suggests that our plans may be thwarted, whether we are at fault for the failure of our plans or someone else is.

Writing

Writing gives substance to our thoughts and allows us to communicate when spoken words are inadequate. In dreams we may learn how to communicate with ourselves in differing ways, and can often make things more tangible for ourselves. To dream of writing is an attempt to communicate information that one has. Sometimes the instrument we are writing with is important. For instance, a pencil would suggest that the information is less permanent than with a pen, whereas a typewriter or word processor would suggest a more technical approach.

X

If an X appears in a dream, we are usually 'marking the spot'. It can also represent an error or something that we particularly need to note.

If a cross appears in the shape of an X, this usually represents the idea of sacrifice or perhaps of torture. This symbol also signifies Man within the Cosmos.

Yacht – *see* **Boat** *and* **Sailing**

Yardstick

The yardstick represents the measurement of acceptable standards, often those that we have set ourselves. Symbolically it suggests correctness and rigidity and sometimes good judgement.

Yarn

A yarn – as in a tale or story – is most often to do with our sense of history, or of continuity. To be told a yarn or story in dreams links with our need for heroes and heroines, and perhaps our need for a mentor. Yarn in the sense of knitting yarn or twine often signifies our ability to create order out of chaos. Many years ago it also suggested spinning, an archetypal symbol for life, and often in dreams it is this image that is portrayed. We fashion our lives out of what we are given.

Yawn

In the animal kingdom a yawn is often a warning against aggression, and a yawn in dreams may be a way of controlling our own or another's abusive behaviour.

Yeast

Yeast is accepted as a substance which both lightens food and makes it palatable. At the same time it changes the substance and texture. In dreams it represents ideas or influences which can irrevocably change our lives or situations, often for the better.

Yew – *see also* **Tree**

In former times the yew tree symbolised mourning and sadness, and the idea of eternal life. Such a symbol can surface as instinctive awareness in dreams.

There can be an aspect of word play here, in that the 'yew' is in fact 'you' in the sense of someone other than the dreamer.

Yin-Yang

The yin-yang symbol signifies a state of dynamic potential. In dreams it indicates the balance between the instinctive, intuitive nature of the feminine and the active, rational nature of the masculine, and our need to establish a balance between the two.

Yoke

In ancient dream lore a yoke was said to represent marriage.

Youth – *see* **Adolescent**

Yule Log – *see also* **Fire**

A Yule log represents a spiritual offering or sacrifice, particularly at the time of a spiritual or religious celebration. In dreams it will be seen as a symbol of light and new life, and frequently is a sign of prosperous times to come.

Zebra – *see also* **Horse**
This animal has the same significance as the horse, but with the additional meaning of balancing the negative and the positive in a very dynamic way.

Zigzag – *see also* **Meander**
A zigzag can often suggest some kind of exploratory movement, or a passage through some difficulty which is not totally straightforward. It may also signify a discharge of energy such as a bolt of lightning.

Zip
Psychologically, we are capable of being either open or closed to our friends and family. Often a zip in a dream can highlight this. A stuck zip suggests a difficulty in keeping our dignity in an awkward situation.

Zodiac
Many people have a fascination with horoscopes, without necessarily understanding the significance. It is often only when we begin the journey of self-discovery that such images and symbols will appear in dreams. Frequently, the animal or creature associated with our own sign will appear, almost as a reminder of basic principles. The way we deal with that image give us insight into how we really feel about ourselves.

The zodiac wheel is symbolic of our relationship with the universe. Sometimes the signs of the zodiac are used in dreams to demonstrate time or the passing of time and also suggest courses of action we might take. For instance, if we dream of a lion playing with a fish we might have to become brave (Leo) in dealing with sensitivity (Pisces). Each sign also rules a particular part of the body, and often a dream alerts us to a possible imbalance.

The spheres of influence are described below:

Aries The symbol is the Ram and it governs the head. The colour associated with the sign is red. **Taurus** The symbol is the Bull and it governs the throat. The colours associated with the sign are blue and pink. **Gemini** The symbol is the Twins (often shown as masculine and feminine) and it governs the shoulders, arms and hands. The colour associated with the sign is yellow. **Cancer** The symbol is the Crab and it governs the stomach and higher organs of digestion. The colours associated with the sign are either violet or emerald green. **Leo** The symbol is the Lion and it governs the heart, lungs and liver. The colours associated with the sign are gold and orange. **Virgo** The symbol is the Virgin and it governs the abdomen and intestines. The colours associated with the sign are grey and navy blue. **Libra** The symbol is the Scales and it governs the lumbar region, kidneys and skin. The colours associated with the sign are blue and violet; its specific gemstones are opal and lapis lazuli. **Scorpio** The symbol is the Scorpion and it governs the genitals. The colours associated with the sign are deep red and purple. **Sagittarius** The symbol is the Archer and it governs the hips, thighs and nervous system. The colours associated with the sign are light blue and orange. **Capricorn** The symbol is the Goat and it governs the knees. The colours associated with the sign are violet and green. **Aquarius** The symbol is the Water Bearer and it governs the circulation and ankles. The colour associated with the sign is electric blue. **Pisces** The symbol is the Fishes and it governs the feet and toes. The colour associated with the sign are sea-green and mauve.

Zoo

Dreaming of being in a zoo suggests the need to understand some of our natural urges and instincts. There may be an urge to return to simpler, more basic modes of behaviour. We perhaps need to be more objective in our appraisal than subjective.